COMMUNITY IS YOUR CURRENCY

To my Selfhood community, without whom this wouldn't be possible. There are over 60,000 words in this book and yet I struggle to find the ones to articulate my gratitude for each and every one of you. This one's for you. x

COMMUNITY IS YOUR CURRENCY

DAISY MORRIS

First published in Great Britain in 2023 by Yellow Kite
An imprint of Hodder & Stoughton
An Hachette UK company

1

A CIP catalogue record for this title is available from the British Library

Trade Paperback ISBN 9781399714693
eBook ISBN 9781399714709

Typeset in Stratos by Hewer Text UK Ltd, Edinburgh
Printed and bound in Great Britain by Clays Ltd, Elcograf S.p.A.

Hodder & Stoughton policy is to use papers that are natural, renewable
and recyclable products and made from wood grown in sustainable
forests. The logging and manufacturing processes are expected to
conform to the environmental regulations of the country of origin.

Hodder & Stoughton Ltd
Carmelite House
50 Victoria Embankment
London EC4Y 0DZ

www.yellowkitebooks.co.uk

CONTENTS

INTRODUCTION

When I was 13, I came across an instant-messaging website that would go on to shape the way I interacted with people for the rest of my life. For years, as soon as I'd get home from school, I'd dump my rucksack on the sofa, sprint to our old-school family computer, connect through the dial-up of my parents' telephone connection and sit on the instant-messaging website MSN for the entire evening – every single day.

My mum would shout up the stairs, 'Get off the computer – you've been on there for hours! I need to call your nan!' As soon as she'd put the phone down, I'd jump straight back on and she'd have to peel me away from my screen to eat dinner and go to sleep.

I was a dog to a bone, even though the majority of my conversations went like this:
'u k?'
'yh u?'
'wubu2?'
'not much u?'
'same lol'
'skl was so boring today'
'omg I know ms salmon is so annoyin'
'yh I know lol'

I'd update my status regularly, soft launching my latest love interests to peers and friends: 'DaIsY 'eRe LuViN ??? *heart emoji*'. I'd spend hours taking a profile picture with my grainy webcam, swooped fringe, peace sign, both eyes looking up to the right corner and posing from different angles, before choosing one out of the 187 options I'd taken.

As my teen years went on, my friends and I would spend Friday nights at sleepovers exchanging ridiculous made-up ghost stories, gossiping about school and falling into YouTube holes where we'd watch the first generation of creators' spoof comedy videos and leave fan-girl comments underneath their videos. As I progressed through upper school, I went on to spend my spare time crafting my Bebo profile and even learnt basic coding and CSS so that I could act like the top dog, customise my page and impress my school friends with Comic Sans themes and sparkly backgrounds on my curated digital profile. I'd spend hours updating it; something about it felt therapeutic.

As I grew older, I went on to use social media to stay in touch with friends and family as I left home to go to university where, in between foam parties, Jägerbombs and inhaling Pot Noodles, I went on to secure a degree in Fashion Communication. It was there that I learnt that foam parties are in fact fresh hell and Jägerbombs are never a good idea, but also the role that social media had to play in building a brand in the online space.

I spent hours in the library reading articles and trend reports on the evolution of social media – there were hardly any books about social media at that point because the whole space was moving so fast (and continues to do so today). I was that eager beaver who would wait outside the library at 8am until it opened and, by the time I came up for air, it was pitch-black outside. I was fascinated by the concept of social media marketing and wrote my dissertation on the cultural impact that social media has on our lives and when marketing to different demographics.

You see, I'm part of the generation that knew life before social media – the days when you'd have to top up your Nokia 3310 and set your ringtone to a paid-for polyphonic one. I'm also part of the same generation that can't imagine life without social media; the ones who panic more about losing their phone than their dignity on a night out.

Over time, I've obsessively observed how different platforms emerge into popularity, peak in usage and lose their users to new and more exciting ones.

I've curated my own digital profiles and watched others do the same.

I've seen how brands have catapulted their way to success through creating innovative campaigns and nurturing their communities online.

I've been a spectator watching how social media has shaped the evolution of our culture through smartphones and hashtags (#s).

After I graduated from university, confused about life and the real world, I went on to work in-house for fashion brands, creative agencies and a few start-ups. I always had roles in social media and digital marketing, and was able to apply my years of observation and fascination to different brand strategies.

From art-directing photoshoots to analysing campaign performance, I've been obsessed with the entire process of social media for as long as I can remember. I loved seeing my clients' accounts grow, watching my friends' side hustles evolve into full-time businesses and seeing my colleagues' passion projects become sustainable and monetisable brands.

But here's a secret that I'll let you in on: I spent the first four years of my career feeling intense anxiety and limiting beliefs surrounding my own abilities. I struggled with this lingering feeling that I was 'winging it' and I would find myself scouring the internet for hours, searching for blogs, vlogs or any type of resource I could get my hands on, to 'upskill'. Eventually, after overloading my mind with endless amounts of information, I would inevitably lead myself into a downward spiral and end up staring into space, fantasising about becoming a tree surgeon or walking Pomeranians for a living.

It's safe to say that I know that social media can be incredibly overwhelming at times – I've been there and experienced it. That's exactly why I'm so committed to changing that. **It's time to reframe the way we think about social media, for our businesses and for ourselves.**

To give you the backstory on why I'm writing this book, before I founded The Selfhood (a social media consultancy and online community), I was in fashion and events, working within a. alongside big digital marketing and social media agencies. You know the type – the ones with ping-pong tables in the break-out area, kombucha stacked in the fridge, Scandi furniture scattered around the office and a 'you're-not-cool-enough-to-be-here' playlist subtly playing in the background. They were the kinds of spaces that would eventually trigger you into cutting an 'edgy bob' in a bid to 'fit in' and leave you in a state of immediate and unfathomable regret (yes, I am talking from experience!).

There were times when, after receiving a weekly or monthly report filled with what I believed to be totally unnecessary jargon and acronyms, I would stare at the wall and think to myself, 'Why do people make this so hard?' Luckily enough, I was able to make sense of the jargon thrown my way, but I also understood that if anyone else was to look at my laptop and attempt to decipher what was on the screen, they may as well have been reading hieroglyphs.

Around the same time I was working with said agencies, a few uni mates and old friends were starting their own creative side hustles, businesses or trying to break into the creator world. We'd meet for wine and pizza and they'd confess their struggles with social media, explaining that they felt the whole 'growing a following' thing was really difficult and, frankly, quite over-whelming. I knew there had to be a space to decipher the hiero-glyphs and make it all a little less intimidating.

Throughout that time I'd also been listening to a business podcast (one of the good ones, I promise!) called *How I Built This*. The premise was simple: two entrepreneurs interviewed amazing business owners about their journey. One particular episode was an interview with Whitney Wolfe Herd, diving into her journey with the dating app, *Bumble*, known for its focus on women's safety.

As Whitney spoke about her failures and triumphs, I decided enough was enough. I had more to offer – I knew it. I handed in my notice that day, with no savings and no back-up plan, but enough fire in my belly to sustain me and the knowledge that I was ready for a change.

The thing is, despite the challenging times in my early career, I saw the immense potential in social media. I'd watched communities blossom, brands transform overnight and creators become household names. After countless experiences of being made to feel really ignorant for asking questions and challenging the jargon that came with the world of digital marketing and social media, I made it my mission for The Selfhood to be an inclusive space where no question was ever too big or too small. I wanted people to experience social media and digital marketing in a way that wasn't always focused on numbers and vanity metrics, but how it's supposed to be – as something that connects us, unites us and helps us bring positivity to the world.

But then I realised that I was going to have to learn to promote myself and my business online. It felt like that dream where you're on a stage naked and forget your lines and the audience starts throwing tomatoes at you and calling you a massive loser, only this time it was real. It felt so exposing; I had no idea where to begin. I worked in marketing and helped brands and businesses cultivate their own stories and followings, but having to promote my own business? Forget about it. Showing up on camera? Nope. Bye. C ya.

The reality was I didn't have a choice, so I did it – I put myself out there. As a result of pushing through the initial cringe I felt, I've been able to grow my own community, without which I wouldn't be writing this book and sharing my learnings with you. I wouldn't be hosting events, getting the chance to work with my favourite brands on their community growth strategies and, most importantly, I wouldn't have the incredible URL and IRL connections that I get to experience today.

So, I wanted to write the book I wish I'd read when starting my own journey. Maybe you have a community and you feel things have stagnated and you feel lost on where to take things next. Perhaps you have a solid community and you want an injection of ideas to help you elevate it. It could be that you're at the beginning of your journey and you're looking to find a social media pal to support you on your way. Either way, I'm going to share my failures and lessons and everything I know about how to grow a thriving community, so that you can build something meaningful of your own.

I will teach you how to magnetise your very own community and following in the same way that I teach my clients, collaborators and my own community. I truly believe that this knowledge will give you the tools and confidence to get your magic out there, find your people and create something long lasting.

Your community is your currency, fact.

Quite frankly, I'm sick of seeing talented people with big dreams and incredible ideas stop short of putting themselves out there online for fear of what Sally-Anne from Year 5 might think. I'm here to help you bring your vision to life.

So, what can you expect? Above all else, a human, patient and clear approach – we're in this together and I'm going to teach you everything I know in a digestible and jargon-free zone. There's also a resources hub on my website – www.theselfhood. com/communityisyourcurrencyresources – with PDF work-sheets for you to download as 'extras' to really cement the tools you'll be learning as we go.

As someone who has been trolled multiple times, I know first-hand how social media can leave you feeling overwhelmed, how comparison culture can seep in and how scrolling and swiping can give you that sinking feeling that you're simply not enough and lead to posting paralysis (see page 131).

So, I want us to say goodbye to that, together. I want you to feel a full-body YES about marketing your business, creative work or side hustle. I want you to fully understand the strategies, including the why and the how. I want you to laugh along the way, to feel included in the process and, ultimately, feel part of a community.

My personal journey into community-building came with challenges and road blocks that were tricky to navigate at times. I'll share my own embarrassing moments and failures happily because I know all too well that shared experience is one of the best ways to learn – it's always about collaboration, not competition, and realness is far too long overdue. But I also want to acknowledge that my experience has come with many privileges. I am a white, heterosexual, non-disabled woman who had the privilege of going to university and was afforded the luxury of being able to live in a capital city. I am not naive as to how this will have impacted my experience. However, I still believe there are valuable lessons in some of the difficulties I faced throughout my journey.

This is not a 'growth hacking' book about growing millions of followers who sit on the fence about your business. It's a book about creating a meaningful community of fans who root for you, advocate for you and help you build a purpose-led and long-lasting business. Feel free to write on the pages that follow, stick in Post-It notes as tabs and journal your thoughts as we go through this together.

So, if you're ready to share your overflowing potential and glass-ceiling-breaking vision with the rest of the world, let's do this.

Chapter 1

THE IMPORTANCE OF COMMUNITY

'We have always needed people around us in order to help us actualise both our physical and emotional needs. In today's society, having a virtual or IRL community allows us to play out and experiment with our identity, receive emotional security and affirmation, as well as have access to various resources to help our survival and movement through life.'

Tasha Bailey, psychotherapist
and founder of online community
RealTalk.Therapist

In this first chapter, I'm going to break down the difference between an audience and a community, and walk you through my 'three Cs' of community-building which will act as a framework for your future strategy. But first, I want to give you a bit more background on my journey into growing my own online tribe and business network.

MY JOURNEY INTO COMMUNITY

Several years ago, I decided to move to London. I had no connections there, no network and no cool cliques mentioning my name at parties, but I needed to escape my sleepy home town and get myself out into the big wide world. I got a job in digital marketing, took the plunge and moved.

Very quickly I learnt that making friends as an adult in a brand-new city was going to be pretty hard. When you're at school, you see your friends every day; you go to class together, eat lunch together, meet up at the weekend and go to parties, collectively prank call your crushes and get embarrassed when they find out that it's you. Sadly, adult life brings more responsibility. We annoyingly have to wash our clothes, cook and eat food that isn't 100 per cent beige, take the bins out and read books so that we have something interesting and meaningful to talk about on dates.

All of this takes up a significant amount of time, meaning that we don't get the same one-on-one time with new friends. In between adulting admin, we're frantically panicking that everyone else is 'killing it' – Greg just got engaged in the Maldives, Aisha just had her second baby and I still can't even make a coffee without spilling it, let alone a child.

As an introverted extrovert who struggled with social anxiety, I found my first year in London really hard and often debated giving up and moving back home. Despite my loneliness and homesickness, I decided to stick around and it was during that time that I learnt the true purpose and meaning of community. I joined sports teams, went to pottery classes and exhibitions with work friends and attended women's sharing circles where we chanted and burnt our limiting beliefs. I once even trekked for an hour to the other side of London on a Sunday evening to watch a monk give a talk about the meaning of life and connected with some of the kindest people I've ever met. I used websites like Eventbrite to find local events and joined Facebook groups to discover group activities that sounded interesting because I couldn't keep doing laps of Tower Bridge on my own each night, in an attempt to stay busy. I knew I needed to get out of my funk and build a community and find people I could enjoy the city with. In order to do that, I was going to have to put myself out there.

Fast forward three years into my London residency and I had made new friends and started thinking about leaving my job. I was still very much living in my overdraft and doggy-paddling my way through my student-loan debt and, aside from my sad bank balance, the fear of failure held me back. I would look at other women in the industries I wanted to be in who were doing amazing work on social media and instantly develop chronic comparisonitis and retreat to my comfort cave of doom in a job that I secretly hated.

Although I'd built a community of new friends and work colleagues, I had absolutely zero presence online. In the business world, I simply didn't exist. I'd pulled a Houdini on LinkedIn a few years previously because I was sick of receiving cold sales messages and my Instagram account was full of pictures of my dog, cheese fondue and the occasional thirst trap. My digital footprint was non-existent. That, combined with the fact that the idea of going to a networking event and 'selling myself' to a group of corporate stuffy strangers made me feel violently ill, meant that there was a lot of work for me to do.

I had the itch to quit and it wouldn't go away. I lay awake at night romanticising a new freelance life. My dream was to travel and work and I knew this was the only way I was going to be able to do it. On an idle Friday one April, after a terrible week at work, I found myself on the Tube feeling totally and utterly burnt out by my job. It wasn't just the long hours, the 'he-went-to-Elevenerife-if-you-went-to-Tenerife' office hierarchy and one-upmanship, or the unnecessarily wordy emails; I came to a realisation that I was completely unfulfilled, and I couldn't shake it off. When I got to the office, I impulsively handed in my notice.

As someone who thrives under pressure and typically throws themselves in at the deep end, this left me with no choice but to get off my arse and go and find some work. The following Monday, after a weekend of saying 'what the hell have I done?' out loud to myself, I sent an email to everyone I had ever worked with and let them know I'd gone freelance.

I was lucky enough to pick up a three-day-a-week contract, which would cover my rent and bills and allowed me time to work on growing my own brand. I even faced my fear of networking (which is not as bad as you think – I promise; we're going to talk about that later) and, as a result, I managed to pick up more work. I suddenly had the freedom to do what I wanted and build something of my own. I worked on a few really crappy jobs at the beginning, learnt from the horrible mistake of working without a contract, got ghosted on a few invoices and faced repeated rejections. I worked 13-hour days and weekends, and eventually managed to save enough to take a trip around South East Asia while working on client projects remotely.

During my time away, I started to receive messages about a 'mystery virus'. As the weeks went on, the tone of the messages became more and more serious and, while I was in Vietnam, the mask rule was implemented and things began to shut down rapidly. A week after I landed back home in the UK, we went into lockdown. I spent a few days chatting with friends via the *Houseparty* app, ate chocolate for breakfast and even attended a thirtieth birthday party that was hosted in a Facebook group with a live-streamed DJ. Like many of us, I thought that it was a holiday and a chance to put my feet up for a bit – Covid-19 would be gone in a few weeks and normal life would resume.

Normal life did not resume: my upcoming projects, and subsequently my income, were paused or cancelled, and all of my revenue for the foreseeable dried up within a matter of days. There I was, once again, in my overdraft from my trip and with hefty London rent due.

I spent three days listening to my 'wallowing-in-self-pity' playlist and eating frozen pizzas while simultaneously panicking and calling my landlord asking for a rent holiday. After three days of staring at the walls, alternating between crying and laughing, I caved and started looking at full-time jobs. But, deep down, I knew that I had to make this work. I knew I was going to have to resurrect my LinkedIn profile that had been collecting internet dust, work on my visibility and get myself out there, and fast.

That was where my venture into online community-building began. I started with no following or subscribers; literally nothing: nada, zilch. After a kick up the butt from the 'stop-complaining-and-start-doing' voice in my head, I took the first step towards building my community organically from scratch and created my social media profiles.

Since then, it's been a whirlwind and I'm so grateful to have a community that I can share the highs (as well as the lows) with, talk to and learn from. So, if you're looking for something long-lasting and a tribe that roots for you, then buckle up – there's a lesson in store for you below.

WHO ARE YOU TALKING TO?

Before we dive into the ways that you're going to grow your very own thriving online community of cheerleaders, **it's important that you understand the difference between an *audience* and a *community*.** This is key as, quite often, a business has an audience, but what we should be striving for is a community.

Let's break it down:

Audience: an audience is a group of people who follow you, subscribe to your channels, talk to you and connect with you on an individual level. They create a dialogue with you when prompted and engage with you in a singular sense.

Community: a community is a group of people who connect with you, engage with your content and talk to you. They go to the pub on a Friday and tell their friends about you, share your content with their own communities, advocate for your products and services, embed your business deeply into their lives and stay loyal to you. They talk to other members of your community and build connections which you facilitate which, in turn, builds a deep and strong emotional connection.

At the beginning of my freelance journey, I was struggling to find clients and came across an advert on Reddit from a fintech company looking for a marketing specialist. We had a call and I asked them to explain a little more about their business. They told me about their product and I asked them what methods they were using to nurture their existing community and attract potential new members through digital marketing and social media. Their answers were pretty vague and their content was all centred around sales and promotional messages about how great their product was.

They described their audience as a community throughout the call. They self-congratulated their efforts endlessly. It got to the point when I sincerely began to wonder whether it was a sales call and my data had been sold to them or they were going to ask me to invest in their business. After our call, I was intrigued to learn more about their 'disruptive' approach to community-building. I typed their brand name into Twitter, where I found hundreds of tweets from angry customers, describing their experience with the business as 'like visiting hell for the weekend and forgetting sunscreen but 10x worse'.

Even worse, none of the 'community' tweets had been responded to. I wondered if the brand account was perhaps dormant, so I got my FBI on and did some more digging ... aha, it was not. The cherry on top of the community disaster? The business was still promoting its products in between receiving public complaints.

I want to state here that no business is perfect; we're all human and we all make mistakes. There will be times throughout your journey when you're going to mess up, and some problems are out of our hands. However, on this occasion, there were a number of gigantic waving red flags that could have been avoided that we can all learn from:

- The company chose not to acknowledge its customers' frustrations, neglected their questions and left them hanging.
- It showed no remorse for its bad service.
- It continued to promote its business while it had a backlog of complaints, sending the message that it cared more about making money than looking after its valued customers.

Eek ... What message does this send to potential customers who may be researching the business?

Until we really craft a community strategy and put our existing community at the heart of our message, we can't attract new communities and expect to grow. I want you to remember this:

your existing community – your first 100 customers – are your biggest advocates. They are your ambassadors and your best cheerleaders. You'd better give them good lovin' because they are going to be gold dust for your growth. They're going to give you feedback, share your work and talk about you with their friends. Your first customers and clients are going to be the ones who transition you from audience to community, so you gotta treat them good and reward them.

'HEY, BESTIE'

Once upon a time, while scrolling through TikTok, a video appeared of a young girl applying make-up. She started the video by saying, 'Hey, bestie, today I'm going to show you my first-date effortless-cool-girl make-up look.' I thought it was a bit weird that she had addressed me as her best mate, but I carried on eating my granola and got on with the rest of my day. As the weeks went on, TikTok comment sections started filling with comments such as: 'Bestie served the goods', 'No bestie don't go back to him you deserve better', 'Bestie, drop the hair routine'.

Due to the rise of 'real' and raw content birthed through TikTok and its instantaneous and unfiltered nature, TikTokers were now calling strangers on the internet 'bestie'. This familiarity is a reflection of the intimacy and vulnerability shared in these spaces. TikTokers have the right to call their community 'besties' because they've worked hard to grow their engaged communities by sharing snippets of their lives and building a rapport.

Businesses now use the word 'community' in the same way that TikTokers call their followers 'bestie'. The difference is, many businesses haven't earnt the right to label their audience a community because they haven't yet created a community-focused strategy. Using the word 'community' to describe an audience is a tactic often used by businesses to appear more 'human' and caring. As a result, the lines have blurred and it's now become a widespread phrase used flippantly and without true context or meaning when describing an online following. Brands and creators will talk about their 'engaged community' when, in reality, what they have is an audience. It gives off the same energy as that infamous celeb couple that gets engaged really quickly and breaks up one month later. Community growth takes time, commitment and nurturing. You have to get to know your community, spend time with them and listen.

WHY DOES IT MATTER?

Over the years, I've managed social media accounts with over 1 million followers and social media accounts with under 10,000 followers. Nine times out ten, when I get an enquiry from a business and ask them what they want to gain from a community-focused digital strategy, they'll say, 'We want to reach 10,000 YouTube subscribers by the end of the year' or 'I want to grow my email list to 100,000 subscribers' or 'We've set a target of 70,000 Instagram followers by the end of the year', and when I ask why, there's usually no reason other than 'We want to grow' or 'Having lots of fans and followers makes you look more legit'. At this point I really want to stress this: it's so much more powerful to have a smaller engaged community of people who absolutely love what you do than hundreds of thousands of people who are on the fence and not truly invested in your business and your big vision. This concept rang particularly true when an influencer named @Arii was unable to sell 36 T-shirts that she had designed to her 2 million+ followers.[1] Sure, she had an audience of millions, but she hadn't nurtured them into a community and therefore they didn't feel compelled to support her venture into merchandise.

The truth is, social media has changed so much and it continues to do so all of the time. As users, we expect more from the platforms and we expect businesses to adapt and embrace the changes and, in turn, keep us engaged along the way.

There was a time long ago when I could upload a picture of my dry-looking Nando's, whack a filter and a few irrelevant #s on it and the engagement would be amazing. Sadly, it takes more than some peri-peri fries and a dodgy-looking pita bread to drive interest now.

Back in the early days of social media, creators could post once a month on YouTube and still grow, and brands could upload a picture of a product on Facebook and it would immediately generate sales. However, as platforms have grown and become more saturated, consumers have become more sceptical about advertising and marketing tactics in tandem. They crave more: they want to feel like more than just a number and want to feel connected and part of a community where they're valued and their time, energy and commitment to businesses are recognised. With so much competition out there, it's our job as business owners to show our communities that they are valued and that we do care.

MAKING MEANINGFUL CONNECTIONS
What this means is that you have an amazing opportunity to amplify your unique story and create something impactful. You have the chance to magnetise a group of people who truly love your product and your work. **You get the chance to facilitate some amazing connections!** So, before we move on and learn how you can harness your meaningful tribe, I want to remind you to not let saturation scare you. The world is big enough for all of us.

As we progress through the learnings within this book, I want you to think about the ways in which you can encourage your community to participate together; how you can grow a tribe of people who truly believe in you and champion you and recommend you to their own communities. The businesses that invest in growing meaningful conversations are the ones that stick around for the long haul. Let's take IKEA for example. It has a whole Co-Creation lab which sparks conversations on social media about living with pets, holds feedback sessions on prototypes and creates a constant feedback loop where it asks for suggestions from its community based on their lifestyle and motivations.[2] On the flip side, time and again I have seen brands, businesses and creators that haven't spent time effectively harnessing a truly invested community fail.

Remember, it doesn't matter if you don't have tens of thousands fans and followers yet! Don't ever let those metrics make you feel inferior; I always say **it's about quality over quantity**.

THE POWER OF THE MODERN COMMUNITY

The year 2020 completely changed the way brands attracted new audiences and nurtured them into communities. The way users interacted with social media channels flipped on its head as a result of the global Covid-19 lockdowns; suddenly we were all sitting at home in our pyjamas, unsure what day of the week it was while consuming content at a record-breaking high and questioning our entire existence and what we truly cared about. Days merged into one and we fled to our phones to escape. As our collective introspection took place, we had more content to consume than ever before.

In tandem with the UK lockdown and increased scrolling time, the George Floyd tragedy prompted current and existing employees of companies to come forward and share their experience of racial prejudice in the workplace and, as a result, became a catalyst for conversations and questions between brands and their communities. Consumers began asking questions about businesses' values and businesses were expected to share how they were going to do better for the world, their employees and their communities – and rightly so. With so much choice available to us now as consumers, we want to know where our hard-earnt money is going and we want to invest it into businesses that have morals, stand for important causes and are committed to doing better, not just externally, but internally too. One study revealed that 61 per cent of consumers said they are more likely to shop with a company that treats its employees well.[3]

Before the global pandemic, social media was a place we'd log on to, stalk our old school friends' wedding pictures, maybe take a peep at our ex's new squeeze, upload our snazzy holiday snaps, watch a flat-pack furniture tutorial and share memes with our friends. Businesses would use the space to share updates and show off new products and services; it was a primary marketing tool. Although some brands were using the channels to be slightly more disruptive and create conversations, the majority were using it as a space to sell. But Covid-19 changed everything.

Throughout the pandemic, businesses had to increase their dialogue with their communities in order to stay visible. With the closure of retail stores and in-person events, many businesses had to establish or increase their presence online to reach their communities. My hospitality clients went from IRL wine bars to delivering e-commerce experiences with virtual wine tastings; my fashion clients pivoted collections to suit the 'loungewear' boom and ran interactive livestreams showcasing new collections and live shopping instead of in-store previews; my service-provider clients hosted live Q&As via Zoom; and my musician clients switched from in-person events to livestreams that their fans could interact with. Suddenly, our favourite businesses and creators were at our fingertips and ready to talk to us in ways we hadn't imagined before.

This trend in ongoing dialogue has continued and we're now using the online space in a completely different way: we use social media to learn, have conversations and research businesses. With this major shift in our behaviour, brands have had to pivot their strategies, and fast. Many businesses began using Messenger and WhatsApp to maintain conversation and service with their communities and, as a result, we still expect this immediacy.

When thinking about your own community strategy, I'd love for you to factor this in and start to think about how you plan to maintain and manage conversations. Community management (responding to your community, facilitating conversations) is one of my favourite parts of community growth, and I've dedicated a whole chapter to it later in the book (Chapter 9), but it's important that you're aware as we progress that facilitating continuous conversations is key.

THE ART OF BALANCED CONVERSATION

When I was 16 I decided I was a vegetarian and, ironically, got my first job working on the meat and fish counter at a supermarket. I had to be there at 6am every Saturday to set up the counter, load it with ice and lay out the fish. Aside from starting at an unholy hour and leaving smelling like an old tin of tuna, I also had a challenging colleague who I'm going to call Vicky. Vicky would come into work late, talk over me, yawn whenever I spoke and never show an inch of interest in my life. I would spend every Saturday enduring the latest drama in her life and listening to her complain about her boyfriend, never getting a word in edgeways. It was the worst.

After my stint in gutting fish, I went on to work as a waitress in a restaurant while I was at college, which was where I met Michelle and observed her charismatic energy. Michelle was funny, charming and couldn't have been more enthusiastic about the guests in the restaurant. She would always greet them with a sincere smile and address them by their first name with open arms. She would ask how they were and genuinely want to know the answer. Michelle would remember intricate details like the guests' children's and pets' names. She would always ask how their experience was and apologise and address any complaints quickly and efficiently. Everyone loved Michelle and spoke highly of her when she wasn't around. She made me feel part of the team and would always be sure to introduce me to regulars I hadn't met before and include me in conversations.

We can learn a thing or two from Michelle:

- Treat your customers like individuals and don't assume they're all the same.
- Ask questions and get to know them beyond the surface level.
- Get their feedback regularly and implement it.
- Own up to mistakes and rectify them quickly.
- Show enthusiasm and gratitude for their loyalty.

- Let them be part of the conversation.
- Don't be a Vicky.

Community-building online is very similar to community-building offline: it's a two-way street and listening is just as important as interacting. **Never stop being curious.**

When thinking about your community, it's important to remember to treat your communication the same as you would with a real-life conversation. I'm sure you have enough self-awareness to know that sitting at the dinner table and reeling off every single life achievement down to winning the egg-and-spoon race in Year 2, is going to get pretty dull and annoying after a while, so why would it be any different for your business?

When thinking about your content moving forward, I want you to continue to ask yourself: am I a Vicky or a Michelle? Talking about your business, your achievements and selling yourself is still a crucial part of your community-growth strategy, but it's important to take the 80/20 rule, aka give to your community and add value through 80 per cent of your content and sell with the other 20 per cent.

80 per cent giving: value, humour, behind-the-scenes, educational, inspiring and conversational content.

20 per cent selling your business.

We're going to talk through your content pillars and how you deliver your message in Chapter 6, but, for now, I want you to embody Michelle and start thinking about how you can make your community feel extra special.

Tip: when you're planning your content, use the content planner provided in the resources hub. In the column titled 'post purpose', write down whether the post is there to sell, add value, provide humour, behind-the-scenes content, inspiring content or conversational content and work out whether your content is on track to stay in line with the 80/20 rule.

THE THREE CS OF COMMUNITY GROWTH

Hopefully by now you're beginning to understand why vanity metrics, such as number of followers and subscribers, aren't the be-all and end-all of growth and you can see that a loyal and engaged community of people who champion you is where the real magic happens.

Over the last decade, I've watched the rise (and fall) of many communities and have obsessed over the details of the strategies different businesses have implemented to grow their own successful tribe. I've watched creators grow at rocket speed, and others fizzle out because they haven't managed to differentiate themselves and truly understand what it takes to grow a real community. I've analysed businesses and creators, monitored platforms and watched new features take off and fall away as users ran to engage or let them fall by the wayside. Throughout this time I've pinned successful community-building on what I call the 'three Cs'. We'll explore all of these in detail in the chapters that follow, but, for now, here are the headlines:

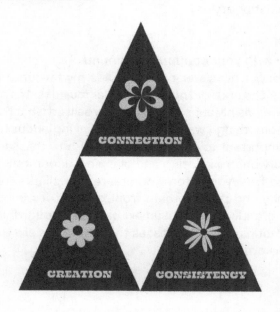

CONNECTION

Facilitating conversations

It doesn't matter how pretty your business looks, no one wants to talk to a brick wall. Create space within your digital channels to facilitate meaningful on- and offline conversations between you and your community while allowing them to also connect with each other and bond over shared interests and desires.

Community participation

Have you ever tried to play hide-and-seek alone? I'm going to assume no, because, firstly, it would be weird, but also it would be really boring. Give your community the opportunity to get involved and participate by sharing thoughts around developments and progression in your business, products and services. This is always going to provide value: give, give, give value before asking for anything in return.

Varied connectivity points

Create a variety of places that live within your community ecosystem – such as social media, blogs, email and intimate spaces – that members can engage with and reach you on (one-on-one and in groups), depending on their preferred communication styles.

CREATION

Creating with your community in mind

I once bought my sister tickets to see my favourite band for Christmas. She and I did not have similar music tastes back then and she was visibly annoyed when she realised what I'd done: I'd bought something I wanted without thinking about her. That's why it's important to always ask yourself how this serves your community before ideating and planning, understanding what they need from you before you create. As well as serving your community and putting them front of mind, it's important to find your creative flow. Consumers can see through inauthentic growth tactics – the businesses that stand out are those that dare to be creative.

Continuing to innovate

The most damaging mentality you can adopt when growing a community is 'We've always done it this way and it's always worked for us.' Continuing to trial new things is key to keeping your community engaged and in it for the long haul.

Embracing new features

Never shy away from embracing new features, particularly those that facilitate connection and participation. Be the leader in your industry and the first to try and you will be rewarded.

CONSISTENCY
Staying on brand

From your visuals to your messaging, ensure your community is always aligned with your mission and pursuit and how it impacts their lives and positively influences their purchasing decisions.

Consistently communicating

Find a rhythm and workflow that you can stick to, creating a schedule that is realistic to execute with the resource that you have available. Consistency is not about posting 14 times a day for the sake of visibility; it's about creating content that consistently aligns with your values *and* your community's.

Consistently aspiring to improve

Complacency is the killer of growth. Review your performance, be honest with yourself and look at your analytics to understand where your key opportunities sit. This will be paramount to understanding where to elevate and the journey you'll take your community on next.

As we move through the rest of this book and learn the ways in which you can start to nurture your own blossoming community, I would love for you to start thinking about the three Cs of community growth for your own business. Within the next chapter, we're going to uncover your values and what you stand for – this will also help you contextualise your three Cs moving forward.

CHAPTER RECAP

- Can you now summarise the difference between an audience and a community? Start to use this insight when you're using social media and observe how other businesses are doing it. Are they encouraging conversations or interacting with their audience on a singular level?
- Moving forward, when planning your content, remember to give 80 per cent value (as a minimum) through your content and sell with the remaining 20 per cent.
- Looking at your existing content (if you have any), are you fostering an audience or a community?
- Come back to the three Cs of connection, creation and consistency before you start creating your content.

Chapter 2

KNOW WHAT YOU STAND FOR

> '**When people relate to something, it makes them feel connected and valued and a part of something. Being vocal about your values is you reaching out that olive branch for other people to connect with.'**
>
> **Ellie Middleton, autistic and ADHD creator and founder of the (un)masked community**

This chapter will cover how you can find your personal style and become clear on who you are. We'll dig into finding your why and identifying your values and purpose, and I'll also talk you through the importance of branding online and clearly communicating your individual vision.

UNCOVERING YOUR SELFHOOD

Selfhood definition: the quality that constitutes one's individuality; the state of having an individual identity.

When I was at school, I had absolutely no idea what I wanted to do. That was, until I found my art teacher – Mr Matthews – and art soon became my favourite subject. I would spend every lunch break in the art room and pore over books about photography, and visit art exhibitions on my birthday. I owe my interest and probably my career within the creative industry to Mr Matthews. Mr Matthews was a northern man who wore funny old-fashioned clothes that looked tired and worn out. He played The Velvet Underground subtly in the background in our lessons to 'help us *feel* and get *inspired*' and made weird noises when he opened a new set of crayons because he 'loved the smell'. Mr Matthews spoke with such passion about art that it was totally infectious. His mission was to help his students see the world in a different way. He taught us that art was subjective and that it was important to find the art we liked to help us craft a sense of self and explore what made us different. He gave us autonomy over our opinions (which is rare in school) and, despite his unconventional approach to life and clothing, we all admired and respected him. He was completely himself at all times and never strayed from his identity and personality – he was as pure as they get. I'll never forget Mr Matthews; he was the first person I ever met who showed me how wonderful it was to live unapologetically.

Your community is going to remember you for the same reasons: knowing your true selfhood and showing them your world. When Mr Matthews asked us to be quiet and get our heads down in exchange for his compassion and enthusiasm, we did it, because he'd given us so much. When you ask your community to sign up or make the sale, providing you've given them the same value, they'll be more inclined to support your ask too.

Your business should be treated as if it's a person. Often, the characteristics we admire in people are the same that we admire in businesses:

- trustworthiness
- a unique personality
- being able to see ourselves in them
- they make us feel good

As part of my onboarding process with new clients, I ask them to describe their business to me as if it were a person so that I can start to gauge the human element of their brand and how they want to be perceived on a personal level. Every single time, without fail, they reel off their own, or their team's, character traits. Why is this? Because people make a business. **Your personal values or your team's will contribute towards your overall mission.** The uniqueness of who you are, your team and your lived experiences will go on to shape how you share your story.

I want you to think about how you would describe your own business as a person:

- What do they wear?
- How do they behave at a party?
- How do they make people feel when they first meet them?

For the most part, we gravitate towards people who are at peace with being themselves. I bet you can think of someone in your life who had an impact on you, because by being themselves they gave you permission to do the same.

When you think of the most successful businesses in the world, they're doing things in a different way to their competitors and they're not afraid to show off their personality and disrupt the norm. So why do brands that know themselves inside out go on to create such loyal and engaged communities? The same reason that genuine people earn respect:

- **They don't force anyone to like them.**
  Like it or lose it. There's no begging, crying or pleading to join the fan club. You're in or out, simple.
- **They don't feel the need to prove.**
  There's no ego attached to their brand. They know who they are and, if you're on board, you're on board. If you're not, you're not.
- **They're self-aware.** They know when they've made a mistake, said something off-key or hurt someone and they're quick to rectify the mistake.
- **They're trusted.** They make a commitment and stick to it, and have evidence to back what they do.

HONING YOUR 'WHY'

Knowing who you are and what you stand for will become the foundations of your community-building strategy. Understanding what makes you different, why your community should believe in you and getting clear on your mission will help you communicate your message with ease and enable you to create content that magnetises the right people.

Over the years I've had hundreds of conversations with friends, colleagues, family, members of The Selfhood community, people I meet at events, strangers I've met on buses on my travels and women in the loos at the pub about their big dreams and ideas.

I often ask, 'What's the number-one thing that's stopping you and what do you think you'd need to overcome that hurdle right now?' The most common response I get is: 'It's been done already.'

My response is always the same: do you think that stopped Steve Jobs with his pursuit in building Apple? Or prevented Whitney Wolfe Herd from going for it when she created *Bumble*? **The common thread that runs through all successful businesses is that they put their customer first and they put their own unique spin on it.** They're clear on who they are and what they want to be known through every single touchpoint of their business. They're clear on their 'selfhood'.

When looking at the selfhood of a business I break this down into two categories, and I want you to approach it in this way too:

1. Self: you, the individual, the business owner or the ideas person. The human behind the posts sharing your unique sparkle and magic with the rest of the world.
2. Hood: your neighbourhood, your community. The space in which you get to share your thoughts and the magic and sparkle with others.

Your selfhood will be the driving force in how you communicate with your community moving forward. Having a unique, clear purpose and mission is no longer 'a nice to have'; it's a must for your business. In fact, a first-of-its-kind survey found that '94 per cent of consumers said it is important that the companies they engage with have a strong purpose.'[1] *Forbes* dubbed this research as 'groundbreaking' and the first study that directly links the strength of a company's purpose with a consumer's likelihood to act favourably towards that company.

Every single business has a purpose – yours too. There's a deep-rooted reason that you decided to start your venture and it deserves to be shared with the rest of the world! Above all else, if you don't know who you are and what you stand for, how can you expect anyone else to?

BUSINESS, BRAND AND SOCIAL MEDIA OBJECTIVES

Before you get serious about your community-building journey, it's important you're clear on the why behind your mission. Growing an online community should always be part of the higher mission for your business. Social media and your online interactions should not be a separate entity to the rest of your business. All elements should talk to each other holistically.

Business objectives

These are your high-level ambitious goals that affect the whole business. Example business objectives include:

- expanding your product range
- launching overseas
- expanding your client portfolio
- diversifying your revenue streams
- acquiring new customers
- expanding your team
- entering new industries.

These are the things that you want to achieve as a business.

Brand objectives

These goals are about your perception – they help you differentiate the brand from your competitors and create an image of who you are to your community. Example brand objectives include:

- increasing loyalty and retention
- creating a brand that stands out from your competitors
- becoming the market leader among a certain demographic

Your brand objectives should aid your business objectives.

Digital objectives

Your social media and digital marketing objectives should always align with the business and brand objectives. So often, I see businesses treat social media, digital marketing and email marketing as an afterthought and there's a huge lack of synergy between what's happening on- and offline. Your business needs to work like an ecosystem: your goals should be clear and aligned.

Of course, as you'll learn throughout the book, **social media and digital marketing are not just revenue-drivers**. They're about brand awareness, changing perceptions, building connections and *so much more*, and we need to bear this in mind when thinking about our social media goals. However, understanding how the work you do online impacts the future of your business and brand perception is key for success and magnetising a loyal community.

Example digital objectives include:

- increasing awareness among new demographics
- creating a loyal following of advocates who convert into customers
- creating shareable content that reaches new people
- creating content that sparks nurturing conversations
- encouraging advocacy with user-generated content.

Now, with a notepad and pen or a device you can type with, I'd love for you to think about your overall business, brand and social media objectives. Having this front of mind will help you think about your ambitions for your community-building strategy and help you identify your goals and purpose.

Tip: talk it out with someone – verbalise your why. When we talk, we're more likely to free flow, enabling our ideas to expand and marinate.

WHAT ARE VALUES?

This was a question I answered the hard way, during a work placement at a creative agency while undertaking my studies. I was working on a brand-strategy project for a well-known restaurant chain in the UK and, as part of the social media strategy process, we conducted an interactive workshop which entailed lots of questions about the brand's vision to use in how we were going to elevate the business and help them stand out online and attract an engaged and retained community. During the workshop, the creative director asked me and a room full of far more senior people to write down the brand values and then asked us to present our answers to the rest of the room.

I started to make a list of what I thought were solid brand values: 'cheap tacos every Tuesday', '2-4-1 cocktails Monday–Friday' and 'half-price pizza on a Tuesday'. Being a university student with an unsightly overdraft, I saw the monetary value in a cheap night out and a bargain taco, which was something that the restaurant offered. While I enthusiastically told the rest of the more experienced people in the room how great I thought the mid-week deals were, they raised their eyebrows and peered over their glasses while their expressions screamed 'be quiet'.

I was surprised (and a little embarrassed) to learn that a taco and soft drink for £10 on a Tuesday was not a 'brand value' – it was a promotional offer – and, when the account directors and designers started reeling off phrases such as 'focused on food and beverage innovation', '10/10 guest experience' and 'striving for a sustainable future', I realised quite quickly that I had got it wrong and sank back into my chair with a scarlet face. However, I'm human and so are you, so in case you're confused like I was, I'm going to break down what brand values are with an exercise:

If I ask you to think of someone in your life who you really admire, it's likely because they're a good person and the way they navigate their way through life and the actions they take align with your own values. They're honest, acknowledge their mistakes, offer support to those who need it, recycle their plastic and care about the planet.

Magnetising your business community is very similar to how you magnetise your IRL community, friendships and relationships. The baseline for your commonalities is your values. This applies for businesses too.

VALUES GONE WRONG

I'm sure you're aware of fast-fashion giant PrettyLittleThing. It is responsible for dropping over 250 new items onto its e-commerce site every week and infamously sold dresses for 8p during its Black Friday sales. In 2022 it launched 'PLT marketplace' – a place for its customers to resell their goods in a supposed bid to encourage a more sustainable shopping model.

Now, the problem with this is: consumers weren't born yesterday and we knew that the whole thing was most likely a PR stunt, so when PrettyLittleThing announced the new initiative on social media, the cats came out to play and, you betcha, the backlash was pretty intense.

Eighty per cent of comments on the posts were negative, calling the brand out for its performative actions and lack of awareness. It was accused of faking its values, and boy did the social media reaction from its followers (and non-followers) reflect that.

It was a straight up pretty little disaster. The lesson in this is: **your street cred can be destroyed just as quickly as it can be built when it comes to your community's conversations.** You can't pull the wool over people's eyes if you make statements that you can't back up. People will find the receipts. This was proven by a study conducted by Twitter and Publicis which found that 92 per cent of people actively seek out comments about brands, products or services on social media before purchasing.[2]

So, what does this mean for you? Your community is going to be researching your business before they even think about investing their well-earned money. They'll be seeking out honest reviews from other consumers on social media platforms, checking out your LinkedIn recommendations to see if you offer a b2b service or peeping at the testimonials on your website. They may search your brand name on social media platforms or check your tagged content to see if your customers are advocating for you.

If you then go on to contradict your values as a business and a potential new community member finds a negative review about you, you're going to lose out on the chance to nurture a valuable member of your community.

That's why it's so important that, when you're defining your values, they're aligned to who you really are. Making inflated statements about what you care about and then doing the opposite is incredibly damaging to your reputation as a business and your community will see through it! As Greg Hoffman, former CMO of Nike once said, 'The moment your audience can no longer see your original pursuit (and every company is a bit different) is the day they leave you and engage and partner with or buy from someone else.'[3]

IDENTIFYING YOUR VALUES

Values are what help set you apart from your competition, define your brand DNA and paint a picture of how you are perceived inwardly and outwardly. **Your values shape your selfhood and are what make you you.** In our new digital world, our social media profiles act as our URL shop windows: research has shown that 77 per cent of consumers buy from brands that share the same values as they do.[4] This is why it's so important that your community is 100 per cent clear on who you are and what you stand for.

I'm not saying that you need to relinquish all of your weekend plans to start saving kittens from trees or streaking down the M1 to end the fossil-fuel crisis in order to grow a community. What I am saying is that it needs to be clear to your community what you're about beyond pretty pictures and sales messages about your business. They need to know what you truly care about, what your mission is and your higher purpose.

Having shared values is the reason we stay in touch with old colleagues, have bonds with old school friends, why new mothers become friends with other new mothers, why we gravitate to new partners, why we go for post-game drinks with our sports-club pals: we have something in common, we're bonding over a similarity.

In order to identify your brand values and amplify them to your community, you need to ask yourself three key questions:

1. What do you want to be known for?
2. When people talk about your business, what do you want them to say? Write down the key words you'd want to have associated with your business.
3. What *don't* you want to be known for?

The first question can feel quite big and overwhelming, so sometimes it can be helpful to work backwards on this exercise as this will help you shape what you do want to be known for:

- Why do you do what you do outside of making money?
- What gets you out of bed in the morning aside from paying the rent and putting food on the table?

Below are some examples to help prompt your thinking:

- A travel blog giving honest reviews about local restaurants is there to spark a feeling of wanderlust, curiosity and

- inspiration to travel and see it for themselves because its values are encouraging people to be brave and see the world.
- An online banking service may post memes about spending too much money on takeaways in a bid to feel relatable and make its audience feel seen and heard.
- A photographer may post tricks and tips for getting over the awkwardness of having headshots taken to make their audience feel comfortable about the process, because their values are about making everyone feel the best version of themselves and embracing their uniqueness.

As well as the traditional uses for social media, such as discovering new accounts to engage with, connecting with friends and like-minded people, app users also seek out social media content with the hope of being entertained, to escape and to feel something. So it's important to think about how you want people to feel after engaging with your content. Ultimately, you want it to become memorable to your community and that can only be done by creating a connection ... and you create a connection through *feelings*. Research shows that when we engage with content or experiences that spark an emotion in us, our hippocampus (that's the part of the brain which is the centre of memory function) is activated.[5] As Maya Angelou once said, 'People will forget what you said, people will forget what you did, but people will never forget how you made them feel'.[6] Your values will help you shape how you land that emotional connection.

You could have the most polished, clean and aesthetically pleasing content in the world, but if it isn't making people pause and feel then, quite frankly, they're more likely to remember the fish and chips they had three years ago on a random Tuesday than your social media post from just minutes before.

Emotional connections aren't always about getting deep and meaningful – they can be about pulling on memories, making people laugh, sparking a new way of thinking, telling a story … The point is, when you do this, your audience becomes more loyal because they actually feel something towards you – and that is powerful.

WHAT VALUES CAN LOOK LIKE:
- Experience: delivering 10/10 customer service and ensuring customers feel valued.
- Humour: making customers laugh and sparking joy in the mundane of their day-to-day.
- Diversity: standing for inclusion.
- Well-being: encouraging mindfulness and better mental health for our community.
- Honesty: being transparent with the community.
- Support: striving to offer guidance.
- Industry-leading: paving the way for others by taking risks and trying new things.
- Innovation: disrupting the norm through innovative and first-of-their-kind methodologies.
- Sustainability: paving the way for a greener planet.

The above examples are just a few of many; yours will be different to mine and mine will be different to the next person's, and that's OK. In fact, that's the whole point: it's about identifying your unique purpose. I once read a quote by entrepreneur Ashaunna K. Ayars: 'a brand is for sale but a purpose is for life' – and I've never forgotten it.[7] **Your values, higher mission and purpose will define the longevity of your business and take you beyond sales and revenue.** Your values are not just words you use when talking about your business. Your values are not just verbs to be peppered into captions and blog posts. The values that you define through careful and mindful consideration will go on to pave how you magnetise your tribe and will be the template and guide for how you showcase your business online.

In the resources hub there are multiple exercises to help you revisit and uncover your values. Once you have established them, this will help you craft your unique business story.

CRAFTING YOUR STORY

Every successful business has a story behind it. We gravitate towards stories because:

WE REMEMBER THEM
When our brains process stories involving a character, they produce the 'feel-good' hormone oxytocin which increases empathy and connection, and improves memory, which makes us more likely to remember the story.

THEY HELP US CURATE OUR OWN IDENTITIES
As humans, we strive to be unique, and the businesses whose stories we choose to engage with and go on to support act as an extension of self and identity. When we share a post on social media from a business or creator that we like, we're illustrating our interests and curating our own identities to our peers. We proactively seek out 'new' and 'unique' brands in a bid to show our peers what we're interested in.

VULNERABILITY FOSTERS CLOSENESS
Sharing the intimacies of our story, our why and our deeper purpose, allows us to connect with our audience beyond the glossy image of a shiny pristine business. It cultivates a deeper sense of connectivity. Through sharing the ups as well as the downs, we build trust through honesty and transparency. This is so important for creating long-lasting relationships with your community, because, as psychologist Arthur Aron found within his studies: vulnerability fosters closeness.[8]

At this point you may want to grab a notepad and pen or something to type with as below are some prompts to help you with crafting your own business story:

WHAT IS YOUR STORY?

- What prompted you to start? Perhaps it was a frustration in your industry, an influence in your family or an accidental hobby you discovered.
- What is your big dream? Is there a commitment you'd like to make or a specific goal you want to reach through your work?
- When did you realise that what you did/want to do was achievable?
- Who do you do this for? Why does it help them?
- Name the three main things that get you out of bed in the morning for work.

Once you've completed this exercise. Fill in the below:
[Business name] is a _____ for _____. The aim is to _____.

That's the beginning of your story.

It's easy to get caught up in the day-to-day treadmill of chaos when running a business and, sometimes, lose sight of your values and the original mission. You might therefore find it useful to come back to this chapter to help you to remember your 'why', reignite the spark and fuel the desire to do what you always set out to do. If you find yourself lost or feeling creatively stagnant I find reflecting on this work extremely helpful. Your 'why' will not only cement who you are, it will also help you magnetise your community, which we're going to dig into in the next chapter.

CHAPTER RECAP

- Write down your business values: can you bring them to life with a sentence and examples of how you embody this?
- Write down your business, brand and social media objectives. Ensure they talk to one another and you treat them holistically.
- Fill in the blanks: [Business name] is a ____. The aim is to _____.
- Answer the following questions:
  o What do I want to be known for?
  o What don't I want to be known for?

Chapter 3

FIND YOUR PEOPLE

'When in the early stages of growing a community, seek out potential members of your audience online and interact with them. If they're the right target audience, they should think "this is for me", and interact back and want to join your community without you having to sell or push at all.'

Jasmine Douglas, founder of online community Babes on Waves

In this chapter we'll dive deep into who your community really is beyond surface level and you'll learn the difference between demographics and psychographics, along with the tools and resources that you can seek out to research and learn more about your community. I'll also be sharing my unique method to help you create value-aligned content that truly serves your community.

GROWING A MEANINGFUL COMMUNITY

Traditionally, marketers and business owners would create consumer profiles primarily taking into account age, location, gender, income levels and statistics-driven factors to help them piece together an idea of what their customers looked like on paper. Demographic information is still important and useful, and the traditional information marketers have used is still relevant. For example, if you're a local dentist, you'll want to know that your audience lives within a 10-km radius because it's unlikely they'll travel much further, unless you start to offer products or services that can be accessed globally. It may be that your business is only suitable for certain age ranges – like selling supplements for people who experience menopause, for example. However, it's not the *only* information you need to start thinking about when growing a meaningful and invested community.

The truth is, even though they may belong to the same age group, live in similar areas and share similarities when coming from a statistics perspective, we can't assume that your community thinks the same way and shares priorities and values. I'm sure you can think of friends, family, people from school or people who you grew up with of the same age who could not be more different from you. That is normal – that is life – and, especially as digital platforms give us the autonomy to explore ourselves, our creativity, our interests and our desires, that evolution of self-exploration will only continue. **The way that you're truly going to create a meaningful connection with your community is by tapping into their wants and beliefs – the things that they truly care about on a deeper level and help them see themselves within what you do.**

It's our job to recognise that the 347 'likes' on a post come from real-life humans with real wants, needs, desires and struggles, who are all aboard the rollercoaster of life with us.

SAME, BUT DIFFERENT

If you live in or have visited the UK, you're probably familiar with Tesco supermarket, aka the largest retailer in Great Britain. In 2007 the multinational retailer Tesco emerged into the US market as 'Fresh & Easy' with almost $500 million in investment.[1] After six years of trading, Tesco exited the US market at the cost of $2 billion.

Despite spending $1 billion researching the US market, Tesco failed to connect its learnings and apply them to its business. In the UK, shoppers buy fewer goods more frequently and the stores closest to train stations are most profitable. Tesco launched with the same 'on-the-go' approach with stores along the East Coast where shoppers travel by car and buy in bulk to save multiple trips. Tesco overlooked cultural differences and consumer habits and its venture across the pond flopped.

I share this to remind you that even a huge retailer with billions to spend on a go-to-market strategy tanked because it didn't apply the lifestyle habits, wants and needs of its new customers to its strategy.

UNCOVERING THE PSYCHOGRAPHICS OF YOUR COMMUNITY

The first step is to delve into the psychographics of your community and create personas as this will help you craft your story and build out content ideas that will naturally magnetise the right people. Personas are different people or 'characters' who you envision buying from you. Perhaps you already have data on your community to help you craft this – you may be leaning on research at this stage. Either way, creating personas that you can name will help you to create narratives and content ideas that are so compelling that your community wants to embed your offer within their lives because it speaks to them directly.

Being understood and understanding others is one of the most important human needs in life – it helps us feel safe and recognised. By acknowledging your community's beliefs, lifestyle habits and even their problems, and being able to support them, they will naturally feel seen and heard, which is a vital part of your magnetism strategy.

Below I've outlined some of the key factors you should include when thinking about your own personas. You could look to write these down; however, I personally find that it's more creatively stimulating (and fun) to create collages and weave this information together with visuals. You could do this digitally or with magazine cut-outs.

Demographics
- age
- location
- gender (if relevant)
- income level (if relevant)

- occupation
- housing

Psychographics

- **Beliefs:** do they feel strongly about any particular subjects? This could be anything from religion and politics to culture and education.
- **Values:** the same way that you've defined values for your own business, it's important to establish the values for your community.
- **Personality types:** are they big thinkers? Extroverts? Ambitious? Relaxed? Sensitive? Creative? Describe them as if you're describing a friend. What role do they play in the friendship group?
- **Attitudes:** what are their attitudes to life? Are they humorous? Relaxed? Excitable? Conventional? Whimsical? Friendly?
- **Hobbies and interests:** what do they enjoy doing in their spare time? Yoga? Live music? Trips in nature? Travelling to new places? Learning new languages? Imagine their lifestyles.
- **Big dreams:** what do they aspire to in life? How can your business help them get there or aid in their journey towards their idea of 'success'?
- **Challenges:** what challenges do they face in their lives? How could you look to help them overcome those challenges with what you do?

I name my own personas after my favourite artists. You don't have to go down this route, but I find it makes them easier to remember (and it's more fun). I refer back to them when looking at my own community and the projects I work on and think about whether the persona I've created would benefit from my offer or ideas. This makes the personas feel more like real people and it becomes easier to reference them when ideating for new content, campaigns, products and services. I've also based my own personas on my existing community and clients.

Let's take one of my personas – Marlena – as an example. Marlena is a millennial woman living in Manchester where she and her partner recently purchased their first home. She is a marketing director at an up-and-coming independent fashion brand looking for consultancy support for herself and her growing marketing team in developing a community-focused strategy. She has identified the objective of re-engaging the existing community members and acquiring new ones as part of the overall business and brand objectives.

Marlena is confident and nurturing; she wants the best for her team and often has big creative ideas, but struggles to find the time to execute them. Outside of work she enjoys food and travel and frequently visits new cities on a quest to discover the latest vegan foodie hotspots, and even has a foodie YouTube account where she vlogs about the hidden food gems from her trips.

Eventually she would love to run her own business, combining her love for food and fashion and create a pop-up food business catering fashion events.

Her challenges are finding time to execute the big ideas and visions she has within her role due to lack of resources and in-house expertise.

I would love for you to start thinking about your own personas and work on building out their profiles as I have done above, so that when you come to creating a product or service, or even improving your existing offering, you have an idea of the real-life people who you're creating for in your community.

TAPPING INTO YOUR COMMUNITY

I'm a data geek, I can't lie. Nothing gets me pumped like a study or statistic. I know – I am the Mick Jagger of marketing; rock and roll baby. Throughout my career in social media, I have found that being aware of consumer habits and the psychology behind *why* people interact and engage with different brands has helped me make decisions about where to invest my time and energy in my own business.

Having an ear to the ground about shifts in behaviour and key trends will help you stay ahead of your competition (more on this in the next chapter) and also give you a wider view on the bigger picture. Using a mixture of both primary research (interviews, surveys, focus groups and polls that you conduct yourself) and secondary research (articles, blogs, studies undertaken by third parties and reviews) is important when it comes to having a wider view on growing your ideal community.

TREND REPORTS
Reading up-to-date and relevant trend reports from trend-forecasting agencies can help you plan campaigns and get ahead of the curve when it comes to designing new products and services. There's a report for everything: trending colour palettes, boomers' skincare habits and even how people are buying furniture. I like to read reports from WGSN, GWI, Mintel and LS:N Global, and there are lots of other industry-specific resources out there. Many brands even produce their own using data from their community.

BLOGS AND MEDIA
The internet is filled with long-form blog content from media outlets and experts. Many include their own primary research and interviews with industry leaders that offer a huge amount of insight. Typing niche questions and keywords into a search engine (don't forget social media sites such as YouTube and TikTok are also used as search engines) will throw up lots of different written and video content.

REDDIT AND QUORA

These two are the underdogs of research in my opinion. You can look at the questions people are asking about your industry here, observe the thoughts of your potential community members in detail and observe their real-life conversations and understand their pain points on a granular and intimate level.

GOOGLE ALERTS

You can set up Google alerts for keywords relating to your niche within your Google account. If you don't have one, they're free to create. Every time a new piece of content is published using your specific and niche keywords, you'll be alerted. This is particularly useful for tracking your own brand mentions too, so if you're planning on doing some online PR and securing guest blogs and coverage you can track how and where people mention you.

SURVEYS

Conducting surveys and polls within your existing and potential community is a great way to understand their psychographics: their beliefs, values and what they want from you as a business and how you can aid their lives.

TALKING TO THEM

I am such a huge of fan of holding focus groups and I do it often within my own community in exchange for a Q&A and my time. There's nothing like hearing how people feel about your industry directly through IRL conversation: you can understand the sentiment behind their thoughts in a lot more depth and they're more likely to be honest. You could do this with both your ideal customer *and* your existing customer.

Tip: you do have to pay for some subscriptions and reports. However, many of the resources listed have sample reports that are still packed with information and insights you can apply to your own community-building strategy. It's also helpful to look at what's happening in other industries outside of your own to observe any trends or data that could spark an idea or inspiration.

SUBCULTURES AND NICHING

Now that you've started researching your general community, it's time to drill down into your subcultures.

A subculture is a group of people within a larger culture who have something in common. Traditional examples of this are: hippies, punks, environmental activists, comic fans or hikers. However, due to the rise of platforms such as TikTok, subcultures have become more prolific and even more niche than ever. I'm going to break this down below.

Like a lot of millennial women, I spent most of my teenage years being told by beauty magazines how I should look and what was 'cool'. I would spend hours on a Saturday morning turning the pages of magazines, subconsciously planning my next 'era' and 'aesthetic'. From the ages of 12–15 *Teen Vogue* was my bible, so much so that if *Teen Vogue* told me that 'bangs' were 'hot', you best believe I was getting bangs out. Often, due to my impulsive nature, I would DIY said bangs and, as a result, spent most of my teenage years with questionable lopsided mullets and have now burnt all evidence of my teenage existence. Bless my hormonal and confused soul.

In more recent years, social media has become the new *Teen Vogue*. In fact, a lot of people now argue that social media has become the new PR. Social media has completely democratised how we access information and trends and has made resources more accessible than ever before. This rise in diverse content also means we get more access to reviews, opinions and thoughts on our favourite businesses, and that's not even the best part – it comes from real and unbiased people (paid endorsements aside, of course). We're no longer solely relying on magazines or adverts to tell us what we should be buying or how we should look; everyone can have a platform to influence others if they want to and, as a result, we've seen a shift in traditional celebrities and brands influencing culture to the everyday consumer now setting trends and movements.

Social media platforms have birthed a new wave of users who exercise identity fluidity outside of the traditional and firm rules of subcultures: they're free and easy; they experiment. This new way of expressing our selfhood has given us permission to be whoever we want – we get to create a cocktail of different beliefs, aesthetics and interests without conforming to the traditional archetypes. We're here for it.

One study showed that 91 per cent of 18–25-year-olds said there's no such thing as 'mainstream' pop culture any more.[2] Platforms such as TikTok have created a catalyst into new subcultures, driven largely by shared beliefs and interests spanning from gaming, well-being, beauty, sports, environmental causes and mental health. Gen Zers are far more forgiving and open to identity exploration, and the conformist approach from yesteryear is outdated; in fact, it's uncool to be so regimented. Identity fluidity is where it's at.

Gen Zers have been a key driver in the new wave of subcultures and TikTok has birthed a place for people to connect and bond over their shared interests, no matter how niche they are. Are you one of those people who doesn't shut up about your cheese plant collection? Get yourself to #planttok. Find yourself giving everyone in the office the book review they didn't ask for? #booktok is the place for you. Crumbs stress you out? Head on over to #cleantok.

This new wave of [insert niche interest and add #tok to it] has 180d our way of consuming content and has allowed us to dive into the burrows of our ultra-specific interests and find other people who love the same thing. There is a niche for everyone.

WAVE GOODBYE TO MASS MARKETING

Subcultures are now trickling down into culture and across other social media platforms. This community-building method is only going to accelerate, which presents you with a huge, and I mean HUGE, opportunity to craft your specific message, become known for something extraordinary and find a community to support you. The nicher, the better.

I've worked on app launches for Gen Z and millennial solo female travellers and seen brands eat up the chance to partner and sponsor because they're reaching a very specific community that aligns with their products. I've had global brands such as Adobe and Microsoft partner with me to create content for my community because they know that it consists of business owners and entrepreneurs who will likely need their products and services, and therefore they're tapping into a highly concentrated group of people.

Mass marketing is no longer what it used to be; consumers want personalised messages and experiences and tapping into niche communities is one of the best ways you can do this.

If you're looking to find out what your community is already into, you can use a tool called Facebook Audience Insights. This is a free tool that shows you the pages, brands, businesses, music and TV shows that your Facebook audience likes already. You shouldn't solely rely on this data – you should also spend time getting to know their likes and interests by observing how they interact, speaking to them IRL (more on this in the next section) and conducting a mixture of primary and secondary data research (we're also going to break this down over the next few pages).

Tip: join some of the more niche communities and start talking to them. There is a plethora of Facebook groups, apps, WhatsApp communities, Instagram pages, Telegram groups and beyond that you can join. Remember to be mindful of your social media etiquette – this should not be a transactional exercise. Many Facebook and LinkedIn groups ban spammed promotion, so work on building genuine connections and observing how these communities interact with one another before going in on the hard sell.

FINDING YOUR COMMUNITY IN REAL LIFE

Once you've conducted your research into your online subcultures, it's important to get out into IRL spaces and start building your network and connections. This is the part that often fills people will dread and has them turning to me saying, 'Really? Can I not just stay home in my slippers and make content?' You could, but it wouldn't be as effective. There is nothing more magnetic than seeing someone's eyes light up as they tell you about their side hustle, passion project or business venture.

BUSINESS NETWORKING

OK, stay with me. I know most people hate the idea of networking. I also used to despise it too. That was until I *actually tried it*. There are lots of 'cringe-free networking' events you can attend. You can find them by looking on websites such as Eventbrite and Meetup, and typing in keywords within your niche. For example, if you work in the finance and tech space you could search for fintech-related events and find conferences, meetups and seminars to attend.

The great thing about IRL networking for your URL community is that they get to hear you talk passionately about your business.

Tip: don't go in with a transactional attitude. Networking is about the long game. I once met somebody at a networking event and, two years later, they recommended me for my biggest public-speaking gig to date, which attracted many new people to my community.

CREATIVE EVENTS

One of the best things I have done for my business is attending events that aren't always centred around my niche. I once went to a pottery workshop where we had to make a mug with clay boobs moulded on (niche, I know, but very fun – I would recommend it). I got chatting to the person next to me and it turns out they worked for *Stylist* magazine. We exchanged Instagram accounts and I then went on to get featured in the magazine a year later after pitching myself to her.

You never know who you could be sitting with and who may need you. Aside from networking, it's also great to get inspired outside of your day-to-day and learn something new to keep you creatively stimulated.

Tip: before you go to events, have a think about some questions you can ask people without outright saying, 'What do you do?' I've previously found that this question can intimidate people and throw them off. Some alternatives include:

- What are you working on at the moment?
- What's been your favourite project so far?
- What do you love most about what you do?
- What would you change about your industry if you could?
- What have you learnt lately?

FESTIVALS

There's a festival for everything these days: music, wellness, creativity, dance ... the list goes on. You can go along and connect with people who align with your values and connect with other business owners in your space. After landing a gig at Lost Village Festival and hosting a workshop, I stayed in touch with the events programmer and she has since gone on to book me for other events because I made the effort to thank her and stay in touch.

Tip: look for the cultural programmer on LinkedIn and pitch yourself to run workshops or host pop-up stalls to increase your brand awareness. You can do this by searching for the relevant job title along with the company name.

THE BOGS

Get to the places your community is likely to be. Refer back to your psychographics exercise (see page 47) and look at their hobbies: where do they hang out? I once picked up a client in the loos at a vintage resale market on a random and unexpected Sunday morning. A lot of my clients are fashion brands and I overheard a woman in the bathroom saying that she loved the in-person trading, but really struggled to grow her social media following and e-commerce store. I asked her a few questions and offered some friendly advice. We exchanged Instagram handles and, a few weeks later, she booked in to do a strategy session with me.

Tip: don't go in with the hard sell. Remember that getting out there IRL is all about building meaningful connections and helping people, and you can then let your content do the selling for you.

SMOOTH OPERATOR

When you're in these IRL spaces it's worth thinking about how you can make networking as smooth as possible. Someone once told me that they were at a networking event and somebody had put a QR code to their social media handles as their phone wallpaper so that people could easily connect with them. How can you do things differently and be memorable when you're connecting with people?

THE SWEET SPOT METHOD

Now that you've identified who your community is beyond numbers and statistics, you can start to work on the sweet spot method. The sweet spot method is an exercise I created to help myself and my clients ideate our content together in a way that had a deep alignment with our business, brand and community values. If you're ever feeling stuck on how to create impactful content, this is an exercise I would recommend.

COMMUNITY VALUES · SWEET SPOT · YOUR VALUES

On a piece of paper or the worksheets provided in the resources hub, write down your community's values on one side. On the other side, write down your values. The 'sweet spot' is the middle ground where you come together and your values are paralleled. You can then create compelling content that your customers feel affinity with.

Here's an example of how this could manifest into content: Let's say a vegan restaurant opens up in a buzzy district among other night-life spots. It has lots of competitors offering vegan options that are all competing for the same 18–30-year-old demographic. From the research it has conducted before opening, it knows that this demographic is interested in music, art and sustainable living. They buy clothes from independent, planet-friendly clothing brands, love attending music festivals and are 'experience seekers' looking for innovative ways to enjoy food and drink. They are also health-conscious and enjoy spending quality time with friends.

Let's break it down into the sweet spot method:

Business values

- Sustainable produce: sourcing top-quality ingredients from local businesses that encourage a green approach to production.

- Exciting flavour: creating innovative dishes that offer something different with an infusion of cuisines.
- Going against the grain of the usual offer: disruptive menus that change regularly.
- Experience-focused: creating an experience for customers with live music, art pop-ups, events and guest chef takeovers.
- A place to welcome all: even your meat-eater friends will find something to enjoy with our amazing substitute dishes.

Community values

- Creating memories with friends: finding a place that will enhance our experience and elevate the occasion.
- Somewhere non-meat-eaters can enjoy: where both vegan and non-vegan friends can eat and still feel satisfied.
- New ways to experience vegan food: seeking out new and one-of-a-kind food experiences.
- A night out beyond dinner: making the most of every occasion by taking the experience beyond food.
- Money well spent: they want to know that their hard-earned money is being spent on businesses that want to do better for the planet.

Content ideas

- Local business spotlight: a video series with an up-and-coming creator presenting and interviewing local businesses about their process, products and produce.

- Amplify the experience: creating behind-the-scenes content of the community events it runs.
- Chef talks: an interview series with the chefs about their latest recipes and inspiration for menus.
- Creative spotlight: interviewing artists about their craft over food and drinks as a documentary-style series.
- Relatable humour: creating funny memes and videos about relatable moments that happen when dining out with friends.

This is one example of how your values could translate into memorable and brand-building content, utilising the power of storytelling to showcase your values and magnetise your tribe through content that resonates. There are thousands of other examples of content that the restaurant could go on to create; these are just a few. However, you can now start to see how values translate into content that aligns with an ideal community and eventually, customers.

As with the 'three Cs of community growth' from Chapter 1 (see page 23), the sweet spot method is a great exercise to conduct and keep referring back to and building on when you're thinking about your upcoming content.

By now you should know who you are, what you stand for and the people you want to magnetise and bring into your community – can I get a whoop?! All of this insight and thinking will help you work through the points in the next chapter, which is all about knowing where you stand in your industry and also how to visually communicate your business online.

CHAPTER RECAP

- Give your personas a name (it's fine to have multiple personas): the more memorable the better.
- Make a list of your community's demographics: age, location, occupation, gender (if relevant), income level (if relevant), housing.
- Make a second list of your community's psychographics: beliefs, values, personality types, attitudes, hobbies and interests, big dreams and challenges.
- Research your community by using trend reports, blogs, forums, surveys, market research sites and plan your focus groups.
- Write a list of all the places you can start to seek your community out IRL. Research where they hang out and get yourself out there and work on your visibility.
- Write down your values and your community's values and work on the sweet spot method to start ideating aligned content that serves your community.

Chapter 4

MAKE YOUR MARK

'What are you actually doing to help and engage your community? To enable your community? Enrich your community? You gotta be honest with yourself about that. It starts from a place of lived experience – you are them reflecting back at themselves. You have to ask yourself: what are you giving back?'

Peigh, co-founder of offline and online community Swim Dem Crew

This chapter will show you how to find your place in the market and recognise where you stand. Knowing this will help you set yourself apart from other businesses, amplify your unique selling point and help your community understand why they should follow your journey and connect with you.

FIND YOUR VOICE

After I lost all of my work due to the pandemic, I gave myself a motivational kick up the butt to get out of my wallowing uniform – aka my dressing gown – and start putting myself out there. I knew that, in order for me to sustain my own business, I was going to have to work on expanding my visibility and start a community. Within a few weeks I had set up an Instagram account, LinkedIn page, website and a newsletter.

As part of my own brand-building process, I conducted some competitor research. I snooped on people who were offering similar services to me and took note of their brand identity, tone of voice, social media content, website, additional marketing channels and previous campaigns. This was something I had done countless times in my previous jobs. However, if I'm opening up the honesty box, this time I found it so much harder.

Truthfully, I initially found it quite triggering to see other freelancers and businesses in my space killing it - they were working with amazing brands on impressive projects. I started thinking, 'Well, if all of these amazing established people are doing it already, why on earth would someone need me?' and found myself spiralling into a negative hole of doom, eventually leading to a case of comparisonitis.

COMPARISONITIS DEFINITION

A vortex-like hole we slip into when we spend too long comparing ourselves to our peers and strangers on the internet. Symptoms include:
- increased heart rate
- negative self-talk
- a pounding head
- a burning desire to flee over 3,000 miles from our place of residence and never return.

When experiencing comparisonitis, you may start thinking about the weird thing you said in 2011 at that party, or the time your old school teacher criticised your ability, or the time your ex made a comment that your passion-turned-side-hustle was silly, and you convince yourself to hide away and procrastinate.

Truth bomb: running your own creative projects, starting a business and working on your social media accounts can bring up a lot of limiting beliefs, so if looking at your competitors makes you feel like you're coming down with a strong case of comparisonitis and you're not going to recover any time soon, that's normal and you're really, *really* not alone.

If, throughout this chapter, you begin to experience comparisonitis symptoms, I want you to give the negative voice in your head a name. This is a technique used by many coaches and is something I was taught to do early on in my career. Now, when my negative self-talk 'Tina' pops up, I can tell her to '0121 do one' because I know she's not real; she's just a pesky voice trying to keep me safe in my comfort box. And, without getting all

American Idol on you, the best things happen when we break out of our comfort zones.

At this point I want you to remember this: **the market can't be saturated because there is *no one like you***.

In the sections that follow, we're going to work through some exercises to help you establish your positioning. When I work with clients on this, they often start feeling the comparisonitis, just as I did. This chapter is not here to make you feel bad or like you're lacking in any way. It's a healthy exercise that is only going to make you stand out to your community – I promise.

Let's start with identifying your competition (shock horror – this is actually a very positive exercise when you reframe your mindset).

HEALTHY COMPETITION

When I host workshops or strategy sessions and I begin the competitor-analysis exercise with clients, I often see them get consumed by their competition and start to negatively compare their day 1 to their competitor's day 16,009, and think about ways they can piggyback off the ideas already out there. This is what I call a 'regurgitating Ricky': someone who obsesses over their competition and stalks its content obsessively to the point that they accidentally regurgitate it, eventually morphing into a diluted version of said competitor.

Being aware of your competitors isn't about spying on their every move, catching comparisonitis or monitoring them so hard that you produce the same content and marketing. It's about knowing where you can add value and shout about your point of difference while being aware of what's already out there. It's an exercise that should enhance your uniqueness, not dilute it. Remember that your dream client or customer is drawn to you for you, your story and your individuality. Your story is one thing your competitors can't take from you, so you should be sharing it where possible. As the queen of social media, Kim Kardashian, once said, 'They can steal your recipe but the sauce won't taste the same'.[1]

Ultimately, having competitors is not a bad thing. In fact, it's good to have competition. Having competitors reaffirms the demand for what we do, it keeps us on our toes, gives us something to benchmark ourselves against and prompts us to ensure we're optimising opportunities and upping our game in order to stay ahead of trends in our industry while having a good understanding of any patterns that are unfolding.

Healthy competition also gives us an excellent opportunity to reinvent what's out there and bring a totally fresh approach to the industry. It's important to say that, even if your competitor is marketing themselves in a certain way, you should not be using this as the baseline for how you show up yourself – it may not be right for you based on your values. Who knows, you could even end up collaborating with your competitors, but we're going to dig into that – one of my favourite topics – later on in Chapter 8.

If you've conducted a competitor analysis before, it's great to revisit this task, refresh and expand on it. Conducting a competitor analysis is incredibly valuable no matter what stage you're at in your business. I've used this exercise with seed-level start-ups through to million-pound-turnover companies and it always gives us inspiration and something to talk about. Every. Single. Time. Observing those around you can often spark inspiration, give you food for thought about where you can improve and sometimes it can show you what a fricking great job you're doing.

There are a few ways you can start to identify your competitors. It's important to understand that you'll have direct and indirect competitors and they're two different things:

- Direct competitors: businesses that offer the same product or service as you.

- Indirect competitors: businesses that offer a product or service that, although not the same as yours, could fulfil the wants and needs of your customers.

For example: for a late-night cocktail bar offering a variety of cocktails to suit date nights, birthdays, group outings and work drinks, the direct competition is other cocktail bars. The indirect competition includes cinemas, mini golf, night clubs, restaurants and other hospitality businesses.

It's important to recognise this so that you can start to understand where and how your demographics spend their time, money and energy, not just in the URL space but also the IRL space. Remember, you can refer back to your demographic profiles on page 46 to help you dive into this.

Tip: make a list of all of your direct and indirect competitors to get a feel for what is out there and where your community may be spending not just their money, but also their time. Remember all of this work and learning is about understanding who they are beyond the surface level.

COMPETITOR RESEARCH METHODS

When it comes to looking at what's already out there, the world is your oyster. Don't just rely on traditional methods, such as Google and social media – although they're both great options to get a feel for what is out there, it's important to broaden your horizons and take a deeper dive so that you can fully immerse yourself in the conversations that are happening, not just about your competitors, but also your industry in general. At this point, I really want to reiterate that knowing what your competition is up to is not about one-upping them and trying to 'defeat' them, it's about enhancing your own selfhood.

GOOGLE TRENDS

This allows you to look at trending search terms, in addition to the volume of searches for certain keywords (including your brand name and your competitor's brand name - providing there is enough search volume for both). You can do this for both Google and YouTube. That means you can see how many people are searching for you versus your competitors. It will also show you searches *related* to you and your competitors based on what people are searching for when they're researching you.

You can use some of these common search queries in your blog posts and social media captions to boost your SEO efforts (SEO = search engine optimisation) which is the process of making your website more visible on search engines. As Google Trends will show you the commonly asked questions surrounding your niche and business, you could then look to answer some of those questions with your content (this is a great way to add value through your content too).

Tip: having a good SEO strategy will help to increase your website's visibility when people are searching for businesses related to your niche on places such as Google.

QUORA AND REDDIT

Making use of forums such as Quora and Reddit is a great way to see what other people are recommending to others. It's a hub of suggestions and reviews and a great place to see who and what people are raving about.

SOCIAL MEDIA ADS

If you want to see the kind of advertising campaigns your competitors are running, you can use Facebook Ad Library to snoop on your competitors' active Facebook and Instagram ads.

BENCHMARKING

Companies such as Hootsuite and Sprout Social allow you to pull in your competitors' social media data and see how you stack up against their efforts. It's also an automated process so you won't have to manually input data if you're struggling for time.

RETAIL
If you have a product-based business, you can give yourself an excuse to do the really horrific task of shopping. Look around department stores, markets, pop-ups and shopping centres and take a look at your competitors.

FACTORS TO CONSIDER
When you're pulling together a competitor analysis, there are various factors you should be aware of. These are things that will help you gain a clearer insight into where you sit in the market. Remember, this exercise is about helping you under-stand your own brand on a deeper level, as well as knowing what's happening in the market.

Price point
- How are they pricing their products or services? For example: accessible, mid-range, premium or luxury.
- Do they offer incentives or discounts?
- Are they offering bundles or packages?

Differentiators and unique selling points
- What do they do that no one else can mimic? For example, a one-of-a-kind formula created by in-house specialists.

Social media channels
- What channels are they currently marketing on?
- Where do they seem to have their most engaged community?
- Can you find a link as to why this may be?

Marketing
- Are they working on brand partnerships, with influencers, sending emails or working on out-of-home campaigns?

Strengths

- What are they currently really good at?
- Where do they absolutely kill it?
- What techniques are they using to achieve this?

Weaknesses

- Where could they improve?
- Do you see this pattern in your own work too?
- How can you use this information to drive your own efforts?

Opportunities

- What could they be taking advantage of that they're not right now?
- Could you use this to fuel your own objectives too?

Threats

- What potential challenges could they face?
- Does this affect you too?
- If so, what measures can you put in place to avoid these challenges?

Locations/geography

- Where are they marketing right now? Are they primarily online? Do they operate in person? Do they wholesale or work with other partners?

Culture/values

- Is it clear from their content and marketing what their business culture is like?
- Are their values getting airtime?
- How do they go about sharing this with their community?

Reviews and testimonials
- What are people saying about your competitors? You can search their brand name on Reddit and Quora, social media sites, Google reviews and Trustpilot for this information.

Whether you're an excel Wizard or a pop-it-in-the-memory-bank-for-another-day kind of person, I would highly recommend that you start to document your findings in a place that you can come back to. I personally like using Google Sheets for more metric-driven statistics and Google Slides for screenshotting and analysing content and visuals. I've also created a metrics sheet for you to use in the resources hub which gives you the key statistics you should be looking at when conducting this exercise.

CREATE A POSITIONING MAP

Once you feel you have a good idea of how your competitors stack up against your own efforts, you can build out a positioning map. The aim of this exercise is to help you understand where you are currently versus where you want to be, and recognise any patterns in how your competitors compare to each other. You can then start to unpack how and why the competitors that are performing well are doing so, and get a feel for where you can improve.

I use a positioning map for myself and my clients – we update it every quarter to monitor any shifts in how our competitors are performing and where any newcomers to the industry are in comparison. This is also extremely useful when working on a new business – it will help you identify any key gaps in the market.

The criteria that you compare on the x and y axes should be based on what is important to the customer or client. For example:

- trend versus practicality
- luxury versus economy
- corporate versus human
- accessible versus exclusive.

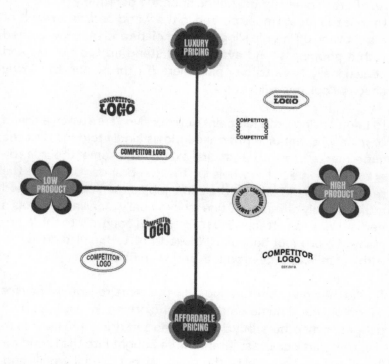

If you're a visual learner, this is such a great tool to use when running competitor analysis. Once you've mapped out your criteria on the axes, you can either create a digital version on your preferred software which you can go in and update, or you can print your competitors' logos and stick them onto a physical version that you draw on paper. I find this exercise is good to do with others, and in person if you can, as it opens up discussion and often sparks new ideas. If you want to do this collaboratively, I would suggest printing off the positioning map and sticking the logos on throughout your session one by one, talking through each of the competitors.

LET'S GET VISUAL!

During a very heated dance-off with friends a few years ago, I thought I'd take it the extra mile and attempt to do the splits in an effort to clean up the dance floor and defeat my opposition. I'm not the most limber person in the world and, as a result of me showing off, my hip slipped out of place and I am now graced with a popping sound every time I stand up too quickly and occasionally have to buy painkillers if I throw one too many shapes. Rock and roll, I know.

I'd been buying branded painkillers for five years when a friend of mine who works in pharmaceuticals kindly told me that the supermarkets' own brands are exactly the same: the ingredients, the recipe . . . the whole lot. The non-branded stuff was the real deal and did exactly the same job as the sparkly branded stuff. The only difference? One looks visually pleasing and has a heftier price tag attached to it. For years I bought into the legitimacy of a product because it looked 'pretty'. I've also done this with oat milk, beauty products and even books.

That is the power of branding – it's the same reason we pay for a logo or brand name on an item of clothing; invest in certain gadgets over others; buy that specific soft drink; and choose to visit that particular restaurant. We've bought into the brand for its values, its personality, the online street cred it's built and, often, how it appears visually. I know that this book is about community-building, not pretty pictures, but bear with me because your visual identity and social media go together like coffee and croissants on a sunny day in Paris. It is important to understand how your brand is communicated, not just through your values and content, but also through your visuals and aesthetic. Having a brand identity that is true to you will help your community visually resonate with your content and your work. It's also what's going to make your business stand out against the other businesses doing what you do, and help you craft a memorable personality, so this next part is very important. Even if you have your brand locked down, keep reading as I'm going to give you some food for thought.

There's a lot of psychology behind the way we perceive a brand visually. From the fonts and colours to the imagery used, the visual identity you choose will largely affect how people view your brand. For example, the majority of medical, finance and technology brands use the colour blue across their logos, communications and social media content (think the NHS, Meta, Nasa, American Express and Pfizer). The colour blue represents trust, loyalty and stability – all factors which the above industries are looking to nail. The colour red is meant to promote excitement, youth and boldness, so it's no surprise that Lego, Coca-Cola, Nintendo, Cannon and KFC all use red in their communications.

I'm not saying that if you're not trying to sell pills or take people to space that you can't use blue, but what I am saying is that branding isn't just about pretty pictures or putting a graphic together and thinking 'that'll do'. You do need to consider how your brand looks externally as this will visually represent who you are, what you're about and how you stand apart from the competition. Think of it this way: your social media channels are your shop windows. In the same way that globally recognised department stores such as Hamleys and Selfridges drive significant footfall to their stores through their impressive shop windows, you have an incredible opportunity to do the same with your social media accounts.

Although some platforms such as Twitter and LinkedIn favour text posts, they still allow the option to include images and video (according to Twitter, tweets with photos receive up to 35 per cent more retweets).[2] In a nutshell: we love a visual.

Trend-forecasting agencies such as WGSN often share insights into trending colours – this is a great reference to look at when ideating new packaging, products, branding and social media assets.

IDENTITY CRISIS 101
I often see creators and brands have a full-blown identity crisis online. I've watched businesses float between clean and

minimal Scandi and vibrant maximalist through to live-laugh-love kitsch identities on a bi-weekly basis. This is an error for a few reasons:

Your community won't know that it's you

Often we're on autopilot and processing visuals before content (research concluded that we process visuals 60,000 times faster than text).[3] If you're constantly switching up your identity, your content will be harder to recognise while people are scrolling. This is why it's important to create memorable and stand-out visuals that will set you apart in social media feeds.

I am a walking example of this: when I first started my business and fell into my competitor-analysis comparisonitis, I made myself a set of brand guidelines and templates using corporate greys with a pop of yellow to seem more 'fun'. It served a purpose, but was so far away from the brand I have now. After soul-searching, I realised The Selfhood as a business was about being bold, standing out and telling your unique story, which was ironic, as the brand I'd created could have been any Tom, Dick or Harry.

I went through a rebrand process and upgraded my palette to vibrant colours, retro patterns and a full groovy seventies' vibe. With almost immediate effect, I started to magnetise my dream clients. I began receiving compliments on my visuals and my content was shared more because it looked more interesting.

It impacts your consistency

Another reason constantly rebranding can be damaging is because it will impact your consistency. What I'm not saying here is that you need a completely uniform social media channel that looks perfectly curated (remember that social media is about more than pretty pictures – that's why we did the work on values!), but you do need to consider that if your shop window looks incredible, but your actual store is a mess, you're going to lose out on footfall and repeat visits and, before you know it, they've gone to your competitor instead. The whole experience needs to be cohesive for your community; the entire journey needs to feel seamless throughout.

It's also important that, when looking at the visuals for your content, you optimise for the specific channels. Check the dimensions of your posts and ensure that you've formatted your content to accommodate the platform's specific requirements. I would suggest that you create templates for the different channels you're promoting on. Then, each time you create a new piece of content, you can populate it and cross-pollinate it through your pre-set templates. This will not only save you time, but also help you remain consistent.

It undermines your true message

Your visual identity needs to be crafted and enticing based on your community's wants and needs. Often, I see people post a picture with a random caption to tick a box. In much the same way you'd stop your mate posting a drunken thirst trap to get their ex's attention, we need to stop posting without consideration and thought purely for the sake of engagement because I'm here to tell you this: you and I both know that your mate's ex can see right through the selfie and your community will see through your ill-considered efforts to get their attention without any real thought behind it too. We always have to ask 'does this make sense for the community?' We'll go through your digital journey in Chapter 8.

TIPS FOR CREATING VISUAL CONTENT
- I'm going to say it again, think about your community. It's all very well creating a super minimalist and sleek brand, but if you're trying to draw in vibrant and colourful people, is it going to resonate?
- Don't lean into trends too much. You can look in to trends (providing they feel relevant and won't date too quickly) by using resources such as WGSN (see page 73).
- Look at what inspires you and keep banks of it (this could be a folder you keep in your phone). Don't just

---

use online resources for this – go to galleries if you can, read magazines, look at your own camera roll and visit Pinterest.

- Get yourself some brand guidelines. You can work with an expert on this or make your own (there are many websites, apps and software which can help with this such as Canva and Adobe).
- Use natural light where possible when filming or taking photos. Content filmed in natural light generally performs better.
- Invest in a tripod if you can – this will make your content look more considered.
- Try not to overly edit your photos or videos: the more natural-looking the better.
- When designing graphics, ensure you don't overload them with information. Remember that social media content is typically more light touch. If you have a lot to say, you could package this content into a blog post or email and migrate your audience out of the apps onto an additional channel.
- Ensure font sizes and colours are accessible. Are they easy to read for someone who may be partially sighted?

To summarise: having competition is great! I want you to keep reframing your mindset towards it and use reviewing your competition as an exercise to help you solidify your own unique spark. When the comparisonitis comes in, load yourself up with a strong dose of affirmation and **remember who you are and why you do this**. Do reflect on your existing brand identity and how you're conveying yourself online: does your current branding reflect who you are, really? And if you're not there just yet, start to think about your visual perception as this will go on to play a big role in how you show up to your community. Now you have the tools to identify where you sit among the crowd and how to use this as a way to magnify your own unique identity, we're going to talk about how you can share this with your own community in the next chapter.

CHAPTER RECAP

- Conduct research into your competitors. Don't just stick to one method – there's a whole internet out there filled with gems.
- Make a list of your direct and indirect competitors and go to the resources hub to download your competitor-analysis template. I promise you, this is a worthwhile exercise that is sure to inspire you and allow you to identify room for new ideas.
- Place your key competitors on a positioning map to give you an idea of where you stand and where you need to get to. This is great if you're a visual learner like me!
- Assess whether your current branding is reflective of your selfhood: do your visuals and identity match your personality? Are you standing out from your competition right now? If not, it could be time for a glow up.

Chapter 5

SHARE YOUR MAGIC

'Go back to what inspires you. Creativity sits in the connections between you and your unique experiences, influences and inspirations. I think going back to the root of this can really help you draw out your unique style.'

Rachel Emma Waring, branding and Pinterest expert

In this chapter we're going to talk about how you can start to share your brand both on- and offline to grow your brand awareness and reach your community. We'll dig into the ways you start to communicate who you are by crafting a killer bio and working on my benefits framework which will help you understand how you serve your community on a deeper level. Before we do this, we're going to talk about algorithms and visibility as there a few things you need to know before you start to share your sparkle far and wide.

CHOOSING THE RIGHT PLATFORM

Now that you've analysed your competitors, it's time to start thinking about the best platform for you to use to share your magic with the rest of the internet. Perhaps you're already using social media to market your business, but the channels you're using aren't quite right. Perhaps you've got a good thing going on one or two platforms, but you're ready to broaden your horizons. Maybe you're just getting started, but don't know where to begin. Choosing your options can feel a little intimidating at first, especially if you're not familiar with the platforms, but it doesn't have to be. At this point, we're just exploring options and that doesn't mean that you need to go into panic mode and start thinking about all of the new content you need to go and create. We're going to talk about repurposing content in Chapter 6 which will help you get the most out of your ideas and spread them across multiple platforms.

I'm going to be honest: social media platforms change a lot (like, *a lot*) due to the turbulent nature of the algorithm and frequent updates to the features, so it's well worth keeping an eye on any significant changes to the platforms that could go on to impact your content. All social media platforms have their own social media accounts where they share relevant updates and inform their users of any news that could impact their content and how to use platforms most effectively. Checking the individual platforms' social media accounts is a good way to stay up to date on this news.

Rest assured, most of the time the changes are put in place to ***help*** **you** and shouldn't cause any drastic upheaval. As we already know, providing that you're creating value-aligned content that serves your community, algorithm changes (I've unpicked the 'A word' below for you) shouldn't have a huge impact on the content you deliver to them in the first place.

WHAT'S AN ALGORITHM ANYWHO?

'Algorithm' has become a bit of a dirty word in social media. However, having knowledge of the algorithm and what it *actually* means is a valuable lesson. I feel I owe it to you to be honest here: I love social media. I advocate for its benefits strongly. But – and there is a but – platforms often update their algorithms due to shifts in user behaviour, which is why it's so important to be aware of updates, monitor how your content performs and be aware of what is performing well. This is where your analytics will come in (we'll talk about this in detail in Chapter 6).

In short, a social media algorithm is a way of displaying other users' posts in another user's feed based on relevance (often based on who and what they've engaged with before) instead of the day and time it was published. The algorithm typically gets a bad rap: often I hear people complain about the algorithm and blame it for their poor performance as if it's a real person judging their content and giving it airtime or not; this isn't the case. Every platform has a different algorithm, but, for the most part, the algorithm will share content based on your interests and what you've engaged with before.

For example, the majority of suggested content on my personal social media profiles consist of ramen recipes, videos of cats doing silly things and the occasional motivational quote because I'm a live-laugh-love girl at heart and that's the content I typically engage with. The ads I'm targeted with are often homeware, cooking utensils and beauty products.

On my business accounts, I see lots of other business owners' content from the industries I engage with most: photographers, other social media professionals and graphic designers. The ads I get targeted with are often from tech or software companies.

The algorithm takes in what you're engaging with and will suggest new and existing content based on this. This is why you need to ensure that participation is at the forefront of your strategy so the algorithm can learn that your content is being engaged with and show it to more people. This isn't a tactic to 'play the game'; just like everything we uncover in this book, it's about creating a long-term strategy that builds trust and purpose, beyond 'growth hacks' and metrics.

But it's not just the platforms that change their behavioural habits – we (the users and consumers) do too. We're able to shoot high-quality and engaging content from our most-used devices: our phones. We can edit videos within the apps to a high standard and business owners have evolved into content creators as platforms develop sophisticated editing skills. This also means the demand and expectation for innovative and engaging content has increased. This shouldn't scare you; in fact, this should excite you. It means that you don't have to fork out thousands of pounds on overly produced content to grow a community. McDonald's, one of the largest companies in the world (and with a billion-pound marketing budget), uses iPhone content to showcase its brand in a bid to appear more relatable because it knows that's what people want now – we want instant, raw and in-the-moment content because it feels more human and that's what we connect with.

WHERE TO GROW YOUR COMMUNITY

Due to the fast-moving nature of the platforms, I haven't gone into lots of detail on the individual features in this section, because, if I'm honest, they'll have most likely changed by the time you read this. As this book is about building a community, I've spotlighted the platforms that work best for this, highlighting some of the features that encapsulate the ways in which you can start to nurture your own online superfans. I would highly recommend that you do some research into the alternative platforms and gauge what feels right for you, as there are many other options that could work too, depending on your industry.

Before you commit, it's also worth looking into the latest demographic and usage statistics as this will help you understand more about whether your community is likely to be hanging out there or not. The best way to learn about the platforms is to go and spend some time on them and observe how people are interacting with businesses and, of course, each other. You'll soon get a feel for whether you think your business is going to thrive there or not.

FACEBOOK

OK, hear me out: Facebook isn't just full of baby pictures and wedding spam from people you haven't seen in 10 years (although there's still a teeny bit of that happening over there). At the time of writing, Facebook is the platform with the world's highest monthly active users.[1] Due to the nature of the platform, all content formats work well: video, text, images and story content. Facebook is typically used as a space for its users to connect with friends and family and, as a result, engagement (likes, shares, comments and so on) tends to be the primary focus when it comes to the algorithm assessing content that is performing well, and therefore boosting it and prioritising it in feeds. So it's worth noting that your content for Facebook should be created with engagement in mind.

Here are some of the top community-building features on Facebook:

Great for facilitating conversation

Due to the social nature of the app, users seek out Facebook to talk to one another (businesses included). There are many interactive tools you can use to encourage conversations with your community through your content.

Tip: use calls to action (see page 94) on your posts to encourage participation and boost your visibility in the algorithm and ask lots of questions.

Groups

If you're hosting group programmes or want to connect your community in an intimate space (see page 123), creating a Facebook group is a very easy (and cost-effective) way to do this.

Tip: think about the topics your community would value talking about together and promote the space as an opportunity for them to connect with one another.

Shopping

Facebook has great commerce integrations which makes it easy for your products to become shoppable within the app. This will help you avoid any overly complex customer journeys (we'll deep dive into community journeys in Chapter 7).

Tip: take a look at the commerce integrations available, set up your shop and tag products where necessary to help your community understand your product and services with ease.

YOUTUBE

Fun fact: contrary to popular belief, YouTube isn't just a space for influencers to share their perfectly curated vlogged morning routines.

If you're planning on honing in on your video marketing efforts, YouTube is your new best friend. It's often dubbed 'the world's second largest search engine' due to its connection with Google and many users go to YouTube to learn or discover something new. If you're thinking about branching out to YouTube it's worth taking a look at YouTube SEO best practice to help with your rankings. YouTube favours content that keeps users on the platform for longer, so it's important that your content engages people from start to finish and your longer-form content in particular tells a story. YouTube also allows you to upload 'shorts' which are shorter videos of up to 60 seconds.

Discoverability
As a visual search engine, YouTube is great for providing information and insight to potential community members about your product or service in a more candid and conversational way.

Tip: conduct some keyword research through Google Trends (which we spoke about on page 67) to help inform your topics, and ensure your video titles align with the demand in search volume to help with your overall rankings.

Building connection
Many businesses and creators use YouTube as a space to give their audience a deeper insight into their lives outside of other platforms due to the intimate nature and 'fly-on-the-wall' feel of the platform.

Tip: include filming content of the day-to-day of your business part of your weekly business admin and make it a ritual – the more content the better. It's worth noting that YouTube requires content (lots of it) so it's important that you document it all (you can repurpose the content for other channels too, which we'll explore on page 115).

Storytelling
As the platform favours long-form content in addition to short-form on its 'shorts' feature, you can dig deeper into your story

and utilise the power of vlogs and interviews to share more about your business.

Tip: ideate a series (see page 117) which lends itself well to long-form content and select snippets to repurpose into YouTube shorts to help with your overall visibility.

INSTAGRAM
Due to the ever-changing algorithm, Instagram, aka 'the 'gram', has been known to cause uproar from time to time. However, it still presents a lot of opportunity for businesses.

As a highly visual platform, Instagram is a great place to showcase your products and services with a mixture of videos, images, carousel posts and longer-form content and therefore present a cohesive digital story. Due to the nature of the different media formats, you can afford to get creative with your content on Instagram and stand out from your competition.

INTERACTION
There are many features within the Instagram app that encourage community interaction – from polls and quizzes in stories through to 'close friends' stories where you can showcase sneak peaks to VIP customers.

Tip: make interactive features a part of your weekly Instagram schedule to maintain conversation and engagement. Developing a weekly series (see page 117) will help you stay consistent with this.

Variety
As the platform favours a huge variety of content, you can afford to serve your community with a diverse range of media formats and display your message in different ways to keep them engaged.

Tip: forward plan your content so that you can incorporate a variety of creative formats into your content plan.

Clarity

Due to the 'portfolio style' aesthetic of the Instagram feed, new and existing community members can easily scan your new and older content to understand more about you and how they can join and participate in your online community.

Tip: ensure that your feed has a level of uniformity to it so that older content can be easily found (see page 74 for more on streamlining your content).

TWITTER

Whether you're into sports, marketing or beauty, there's a conversation happening for *everyone* on Twitter. Users often head there to find out what is topical in the world right now, which gives you an opportunity to engage with trending topics and news that feel relevant to your business. It is a highly conversational platform that encourages participation from both businesses and its audience, and due to the instantaneous user behaviour and volume of content on Twitter, you can afford to be more reactive with your posts as they require less planning.

Listening

Many users head to Twitter as a secondary customer-service tool and, as a result, many brands use it as a space to hold conversations.

Tip: ensure that you're proactively seeking out your own brand mentions and conversations and responding to them. You can do this by searching for your brand name in the Twitter search bar.

Trends

Forty-eight per cent of Twitter users use the platform as a news resource and a space to find out what is happening in the world.[2] This presents a business opportunity to engage with any relevant topics and share your thoughts or opinions.

Tip: check the 'trending' tab daily and see where you can add any thoughts or opinions (providing it feels relevant to your business).

Participation

Due to the conversational nature of the platform, conversation is very much encouraged and businesses often use Twitter as a way to spark discussions. It's also a great space to make announcements and share articles and blogs hosted elsewhere.

Tip: ask questions and use polls to encourage your community to participate. Share blogs and articles with a link for your community to find out more.

LINKEDIN

When I first joined LinkedIn I thought it was for people in suits who wanted to play a game of 'who can brag the most'. However, I quickly learnt that I was wrong.

While, yes, LinkedIn is a business-to-business *'professional'* platform, it's also a great place to develop your personal brand, establish yourself as a thought leader, grow your network and have some pretty insightful conversations. Due to the exceptional networking features and ability to find people from different businesses, LinkedIn presents a lot of opportunity to connect with other businesses and even secure brand partnerships and collaboration opportunities (more on that in Chapter 8).

Groups

There are lots of LinkedIn groups you can join where you can connect with like-minded business owners and professionals in your industry. Searching for keywords in your niche is a good place to start – simply search for the keyword and navigate to the 'groups' tab to find all of the groups within your field.

Tip: don't join groups to spam and self-promote. Use this as a networking exercise before going in for the hard sell. Besides, your value-adding content should do the selling for you.

Post interaction

Due to the nature of LinkedIn's algorithm, you will often see posts from people who you aren't connected with yet – this is a good thing! Take advantage of the networking opportunity and share your opinions on other people's posts, which is very much welcomed. As we know, community-building is not just about responding to your individual community; it's about reaching new people and engaging with others too.

Tip: dedicate time each week to interact with posts that feel relevant to your business and have been created by people you're not connected with, and start to grow your community.

Thought leadership
LinkedIn favours personal profiles from those who share thoughts, personal stories and opinions on important progressions that are happening in their industry. This will help establish and grow not only your reputation, but your business's too.

Tip: turn on Google Alerts for news and keywords in your industry and subscribe to newsletters so that you can start sharing interesting industry news with your connections, adding your opinions alongside it.

WHATSAPP
WhatsApp was traditionally used as an intimate space to send funny memes and cat videos to your besties and family in a two-way dialogue or group chat. In more recent years, many businesses have adopted WhatsApp as part of their community growth strategy. It's the perfect place to host conversations outside of traditional apps and facilitate more personal conversations.

Groups
Creating a group for your superfans and 'VIP' community members is a great way to get them bonding over their shared interests (aka – you!). As we already know, community is about creating meaningful dialogue and facilitating conversations beyond your product or service.

Tip: make sure you have the resources and capacity to safeguard the conversations and ensure you're monitoring for inappropriate behaviour.

One-on-one dialogue
Using WhatsApp could be an alternative for your customer-service process. You can set up automatic replies, shareable catalogues and links to articles and your website to help you manage this.

Tip: ensure that your responses are set up correctly to avoid any frustration with 'bot-like' responses.

Visibility
Sure, traditional social media apps work well; however, you are fighting against the competition and algorithms to get your content seen. With WhatsApp, you get direct access to someone's inbox and can guarantee your updates will land.

Tip: try not to overly spam your WhatsApp subscribers to avoid getting blocked. The same rules apply here – treat your community with respect and don't use WhatsApp as a place to constantly sell.

TIKTOK
Contrary to popular belief, TikTok is not just a place for teenagers to learn dance routines and lip-sync along to sped-up Miley Cyrus songs (although you can still find this content and I firmly believe everyone has to try learning a TikTok dance routine *at least* once – a humbling experience to say the least).

TikTok has had undeniable growth and has become a key player in the community-building arena. The video-sharing app has garnered many users candidly sharing their lives and subsequently has brought out a more 'raw' side to the way we engage with (and create) content due to its authentic and spontaneous nature.

Trends

Trending sounds have been coined the 'backbone' of TikTok. They often come in the form of songs or quote snippets from films, TV or TikTok users themselves. They're typically lip-synced or have a relatable scenario attached to them. It's likely if you're seeing the same sound appear in your feed over and over again (and it's on a loop in your brain before you're about to fall asleep too), it's probably trending. Using trends is a cost-effective and less time-consuming way to create funny and relatable content that aligns with your community's values and resonates with their wants and needs.

Tip: don't jump on every single trend going. Identify if it's relevant to you first and don't solely rely on trends when creating for TikTok – original content is just as important as making the most of trends.

Virality

Due to the fair nature of the TikTok algorithm, everyone has the chance to reach millions with their video content; you don't need many followers to go viral and grow your community fast.

Tip: ensure the concept of the content you produce is on-brand and aligned with your purpose and overall mission. Going viral can be great, but you can also attract the wrong people if your content isn't true to your business. Having an influx of followers who don't engage with the rest of your content and business will result in a lack of engagement and chances of further discovery.

Connections

Due to the less 'glossy' nature of the platform, we're now presented with an opportunity to build deeper connections with our communities with more 'real' content. This is something we know consumers are craving more than ever as trust in brands declines, and people begin to see through sales and marketing.

Tip: know your boundaries here. Remember, you're still a professional business and there is still business etiquette to adhere to. Know where you draw the line at showing off the more raw side of what you do.

Truth be told, there are endless apps available that you can choose from, packed with incredible features to help you grow and nurture your existing and future community. Don't feel as though you need to be everywhere. I need to stress this: **it is much better for you to focus on two or three platforms and give them the TLC they deserve than try to stretch yourself across several and dilute your message**. Let's say you started a YouTube channel and Instagram, Twitter, LinkedIn and TikTok accounts, you branched out into a podcast, newsletter or blog, but, after a few months, you abandoned Twitter and YouTube because it was too much to manage. I could find your abandoned social media accounts, see that you haven't posted in three months, think you're no longer in business and so go and find someone else.

Sorry to sound like a broken record, but I'm going to keep saying this because it's so important: social media platforms are third-party apps, which means they could sink at any time and you could lose your community if you put all of your eggs in one basket. This is why it's important that you also look at growing your mailing list (see page 193) and look into migrating them over to intimate spaces such as Slack, Telegram, Discord or WhatsApp (see page 123). Please trust me on this one – it's so important.

UNDERSTAND THE SENTIMENT

When you do start to explore the platforms and begin thinking about the content you're going to create, it's important you also understand the *intention* and the *why* for people visiting the platforms. Personal branding expert Amelia Sordell uses a great analogy for this. To demonstrate this analogy I've used a margarita party as an example:

- Facebook has a focus on engagement: 'let me know what you think of my margarita party!?'

- YouTube has a focus on learning and discoverability: 'how to host a good margarita party.'
- Instagram focuses on visuals and inspiration: *insert picture of aesthetic margaritas* 'look at my stunning margaritas.'
- LinkedIn focuses on networking and business updates: 'I'm thrilled to announce that I hosted a successful margarita party for my network last week.'
- WhatsApp focuses on conversation and dialogue: 'who wants to come to my margarita party?'
- Twitter focuses on news and quick information: 'margarita party happening – right now!'
- TikTok focuses on entertainment: 'come behind the scenes for my margarita party.'

As you can see, the same topic applies but how you share it will most likely vary based on the motivation for posting and the intent behind your community browsing the platforms. This is worth keeping in mind, especially as you go on to repurpose content (see page 115).

HOW TO CRAFT A COMPELLING BIO

All social media platforms now require a bio. A bio is essentially a modern-day 'elevator pitch'. If that phrase reminds you of cringey icebreakers in a suited and booted room, I see you and I feel you. However, being able to concisely summarise who you are to your future community will also help *you* get clear on exactly who you are too.

WHAT DO YOU WANT TO BE KNOWN FOR?

I'm a social media strategist and there are a billion and one other people out there doing what I do, but how I differentiate myself is by getting clear on what I want to be known for ... which is making a jargon-filled and overwhelming industry feel more friendly and down to earth. My tag line is, 'Making URL feel as human as IRL': simple, to-the-point and broad enough to cover off all of the services I offer, while still being succinct enough to carry over the message.

Tip: refer back to your values exercise on page 36 to help you craft your own tag line.

HOW CAN YOU HELP?

What is it that you offer? Sure, your content should really make this clear, but for new community members (who may not understand your industry or who you are yet) this needs to be super clear.

Tip: focus on the transformation here. For example: 'I help burned out business owners go from overwhelmed to organised and full of clarity.'

WHERE CAN THEY LEARN MORE?

Always add a call to action: what do you want them to do? Shop the new collection? Book a discovery call? Join your group programme? Book a table at your restaurant? Make it as easy as possible.

You can make your calls to action a little more 'fun' if you want to and inject some personality into them, but don't make them too ambiguous, as this will get confusing.

Tip: write down your key calls to action and choose the one that is most important. You can use the others in your captions for your content and alternate the calls to action when necessary.

Some additional pointers:

- It took Nike over 20 years to land on 'Just do it'.[3] Your brand can evolve and change over time, so if the idea of creating a bio feels scary, know that you can craft it and update it as you go. However, it is important that you're able to summarise what you do clearly to your audience

- this will also help you with networking (go back to page 54 if you find network-ing scary with a capital S).
- Don't over-egg it: most platforms have a character limit so you need to be able to chop and change it to accommodate shorter and longer bios.
- Get comfortable with it: my good friend Stefanie Sword-Williams, founder of F*ck Being Humble, gave some solid advice on this: make sure you're comfortable saying your elevator pitch out loud to strangers. If it's something you wouldn't say in a normal conversation, bin it. It needs to feel authentic to you.
- Keep it to the point and avoid 'fluff' and filler words. It's a bio not a novel and you can always elaborate on it when you get chatting to your community.

URL DISCOVERY

My best friend, Kirsty, loves to travel. She's lived everywhere from Ibiza to Australia and her backpack is pretty much her second skin. A few years ago, Kirsty and I booked a trip to Sri Lanka. When it comes to planning trips, I'm more of a 'wing-it-when-we-get-there' kind of person, but Kirsty is the Marie Kondo of travel. Before we headed off she'd created a spreadsheet split into: landmarks, restaurants, bars, accommodation, travel, budget and travel time to and from destinations on a very strict itiner-ary. The trip was a huge success minus some food poisoning, a few blisters and some scratches from attempting to surf. Kirsty knew every hotspot, and we were lucky enough to uncover some hidden gems away from tourists and connect with the locals.

When planning a weekend of fun, it's not uncommon to hear Kirsty say, 'So I saw this place on TikTok' or 'I found this vegan pop-up on a YouTube vlog'. Kirsty uses social media to find new experiences and she isn't alone in her planning style ... Cue fun fact: **75 per cent of consumers research products and experiences on social media before buying.**[4] That is a phenomenal number when you really think about it: 75 per cent of your future community are going to come along via a piece of content, snoop on your profile and make a decision about you before they decide to stick around for the rest of your journey and eventually convert. Even if they've found you through an additional source, such as recommendations, like I have in the past, they're going to consult your digital channels before making up their minds.

This change in behaviour stems from the shifts in social media platforms themselves which were historically adopted by brands to increase brand awareness and simply share products and services. In more recent years, due to developments in the platforms' features and how we interact with them, they have now gone on to become news sources and search engines as well as a method to grow a community.

This progression of user behaviour and leaning on social media to discover new brands is not about to go anywhere soon. The individual platforms are consistently progressing their search features, as they know that their users are continuing to use social media to discover new products, and also to research existing ones too. The Vice President of Google has even noted this shift and, as a result, Google is making changes to its own user experience and in-app features to accommodate the new way of browsing for new brands via video and visual content.

Let's say I'm looking for a business just like yours. I'm typing in keywords on my preferred channels and voila, your profile appears. The first thing I'm going to do is skim over your content and suss out whether our values align and if you're for me. If what you offer feels unclear and I can't understand what you're about after the first five seconds, I'm about to 180 you and head to your competitor.

With this in mind, there are a few foundational elements that you need to be aware of when you're focusing on communicating your offer before we even get into your content structure (which we'll cover in the next chapter):

SOCIAL MEDIA SEO

SEO is not exclusively used for blogs and websites anymore. Many social media sites now scan content for keywords within captions, text and videos. They will also take into account your username and handle to serve their users with the content they want to see based on what they've previously engaged with. Algorithms are very clever and advanced now, so it's important that your content is optimised and that you're reaching your community at every touch point possible, as this will increase your overall reach and discoverability.

An exercise I often undertake is to write down as many phrases and keywords associated with my brand as possible – the more niche, the better, as the competition for more generic search terms is incredibly high. I then start to cross-reference these against the content and captions to ensure that my discoverability is maximised. One of the best ways to do this is to describe what you see in literal form when observing your own content. For example, let's say that you're a graphic-design agency creating relatable content about client struggles and scenarios. Your keywords would be: 'graphic-design humour', 'client struggles', 'graphic-design life'. You should also look to include alt-text on your posts. Alt-text describes the content in a video or image and helps those who are visually impaired understand the context of the content. Although this is not to be confused for SEO, it is best to do this to ensure your content is accessible.

Tip: ensure that your keywords are peppered into your usernames as well as your content to optimise your visibility and chances of appearing in search engines.

AUDITING

I often like to run something I call a 'content MOT', which is essentially an audit on my content to check that everything is working as it should be. Part of the MOT process is to ask someone outside of your niche or industry if they understand what you're about at first glance. Are your values and ethos visible upon landing for the first time? If not, it's time to reassess your content and weave this back in.

Tip: schedule in a content MOT every quarter to ensure that your content is crystal clear to any potential fans or followers. If you decide to host focus groups you could also use this as an opportunity to get outsiders' perspsectives too.

EASE OF UNDERSTANDING

When working with a new client – be it a service provider or a product-based business – I ask them to explain their business to me as if I'm a child and break it down in very simple terms. If a 10-year-old couldn't understand it then you're probably overcomplicating things. What I'm not saying here is that you need to compromise on your tone of voice and start talking in a Key-Stage-2-with-a-side-of-patronise-me-later manner. Nonetheless, it is important to analyse how you're speaking to people and make certain that your community recognises who you are and what you stand for.

Tip: don't assume that everyone knows what you do inside out. A lot of your community may be following your journey because they have an interest in you, yet don't quite understand your world.

IRL DISCOVERY

When thinking about your discovery, I want you to think BIG. Get creative. How can you find your community outside of their screens too? Yes, social media is great for getting discovered, but there's a world outside of our phones that your community is also living in. How can you get creative and get your business out there too? I've outlined some examples of this below.

POSITIVITY STICKERS

My housemate and very good friend, Zoe Mallett, is a qualified life coach and psychologist helping people navigate difficult situations in their lives. She had stickers created in her branding with her contact details on and takes them to events and hands them out as business cards and sticks them around different locations.

REVIEWS

Many businesses with physical locations have gone viral for featuring funny or thought-provoking messages on their A-boards and outdoor marketing. One even wrote and displayed a terrible Tripadvisor review – 'mediocre coffee, wouldn't bother' – with an arrow pointing to their shop. This got people talking, made them laugh and sparked their curiosity. How can you use your own reviews or testimonials creatively? Could you get stand-out testimonials or reviews printed onto business cards?

QR CODES

A few years ago, I worked on an event for London Fashion Week. We put edible rice paper on the cocktails at the party with a QR code that sent the attendees to the brand's social media profiles and the branded # for the event. We saw a huge influx of followers and engagements on the #s as a result.

CLARIFYING YOUR CONTENT PURPOSE

Before you can think about posting any content – and this goes for your website, newsletters, social media, SMS and any other communication you share with your community – you should always ask yourself this: what is in it for the person seeing this? What are they getting out of you sharing it? Your content should have an end goal and you should be aware of this.

The reason that this is so important is because it helps you become more intentional with your craft. You start to create from a place of consideration rather than ticking a box for the sake of visibility. As I keep saying, community-building is about building relationships, and relationships are a two-way street. **You can't expect a community to get on board with you and what you do without giving them a reason and adding value beyond your own product or service.**

By establishing your content purpose, you can start to see whether you're selling too much. Furthermore, you can then identify where you may need to include some brand-building content too. Below are some examples of what content purpose could look like:

EDUCATE

Whether this is about your product, service or the values that your brand stands for, teach your community about what you do in a way that feels authentic to your brand. Let's say you're an eco-friendly travel company: you may look to share educational content on the ways that your community can travel more consciously. How can you get creative with your educational content? I like to look at the less 'sexy' industries, such as finance, and see how they're taking a less 'fun' topic and making it interesting (see page 225 for more on this).

ENTERTAIN

People often come to social media to be entertained. Perhaps they're bored on their lunch break, waiting for the bus or they're staying with their dreary in-laws and want to escape – who knows? How can you provide entertainment through your content and think outside of the box?

INSPIRE

We often head to social media for inspiration. It could be that we're looking for a new kitchen, gym motivation or advice on taking a new career direction. Start thinking about the inspiration your community is looking for in their lives and apply it to your content.

ENGAGE

A strong community requires engagement, and how do we fuel engagement? Through conversation. Sparking engagement comes from asking questions and being curious. Creating content that facilitates conversation is key for this. Websites such as AnswerThePublic will show you the common questions people are asking about your industry. How might you use this information to ask questions and spark conversations?

HUMOUR

There's a reason for the endless amounts of meme pages, comedy forums and comedic Twitter profiles: humans love to laugh! Remember that laughing is an energy exchange – when you make someone laugh, you're building an emotional connection with them, which is paramount to your strategy. What are some of the relatable moments your audience will resonate with that you can create content about?

SHARE

If you're in the visibility phase of your community-building strategy and your focus right now is getting more eyes on your content, creating content that is shareable will help with this. Remember to think about your psychographics here (see page 47): what are the kind of topics your community cares about and are likely to share with their friends and network? This is where your visuals will also be important – remember, the content we share becomes an extension of our own personal brand! Tweets are one of the most reshared pieces of content because they're easy to read and often relatable and inspiring. Take some time to observe what type of content your community is resharing and think about how you can apply this to your own content strategy.

TRAFFIC

After some warming up, you want to navigate your community away from your shop windows (social media channels) and into the main store or conversion points (the place where they can sign up or make a sale) – that could be your website, group chat via WhatsApp, Discord or Slack channels or even a physical space. Using clear call to actions and being clear about how they can work with you or buy your products is key for driving traffic.

NEWSLETTER SIGN-UPS

Part of your community-growth strategy might be about taking people away from social media and into a more intimate space where you can reach them with direct access to their inbox (see page 194 for more on this). It's important to think about why they might do this: what's the incentive?

SELL

It's inevitable that most businesses using social media have a product or service to sell. Remember to refer back to the 80/20 rule when you're planning your content (see page 22). When selling, it's also important to think about why your community will benefit from your product.

Tip: where possible, show, don't tell. Focus on the transformation: what transformation does your business offer? Where does your community start, and where do you take them to? Testimonials, reviews and user-generated content are all great ways to convey this (we're going explore this in more detail in Chapter 8).

You may want to focus more on certain objectives and goals depending on where you're at in your sales cycle or community-building strategy.

SHOWCASING YOUR VALUES

When starting to think about your content, you also need to consider how you can clearly start to communicate your values within your content.

On the next page is a framework I use when strategising new social media projects for clients. This framework will act as a model for you to use when creating your own social media content moving forward.

Using a notepad and pen, or something you can type notes with, plot out the points in the diagram opposite. Your benefits, values, reasons to believe and brand personality will be different to mine and mine will be different to the next person's, and that's a good thing. This exercise is all about shaping your uniqueness. I've provided a few examples to help you contextualise how this could work:

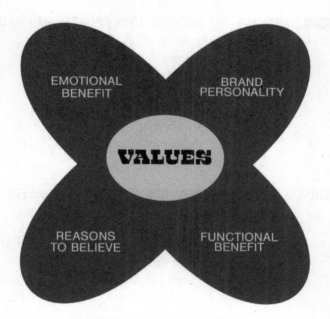

EMOTIONAL BENEFIT: HOW THIS BENEFITS YOUR COMMUNITY ON A DEEPER LEVEL

- Frees up your client's or community's time by helping them.
- Puts your community at ease.
- Supports your community with their mental health.
- Aids them in the progression of their career.
- Makes them feel good when using your products or working with you.

BRAND PERSONALITY: HOW YOU WOULD DESCRIBE YOUR BUSINESS AS IF IT WAS A PERSON

- Approachable
- Laid back
- Professional
- Caring
- Humorous and relatable
- Vibrant
- Bold

REASONS TO BELIEVE: THE EVIDENCE TO SUPPORT WHAT YOU DO

- Excellent reviews
- Repeat customers
- Awards
- Impressive credentials
- Experience to support your venture
- Glowing testimonials
- Worked with credible partners
- Certifications

FUNCTIONAL BENEFIT: THE PRACTICALITY OF YOUR BUSINESS

- Saves them time
- Can be consumed on the go
- Fast delivery
- Quick response time
- Gives them time to look at the bigger picture

Tip: refer back to this diagram when you're creating content. Use it as a checklist to ensure your brand elements are reflected in the content you're producing.

OK, by now you should know what your unique brand values are and who your community is beyond a data-driven number. You should be thinking about where and how you're going to reach them (on- and offline), who else is in the market and how the work you do benefits your community. This is good! We are making progress – I'm excited for you! In the next chapter, we're going to be talking about the content creation process.

CHAPTER RECAP

- Summarise your business as if you're explaining it to a child. If a 10-year-old couldn't understand it, go back to the drawing board until it's 100-per-cent clear.
- Make a bank of keywords and be sure to weave them into your captions, bios and video content. This is going to hugely increase your chances of being seen.
- Start to think about how you can get creative with how you share your magic offline too.
- Be sure to use the values framework on page 103 as a reference when selling your work.

Chapter 6

THE CONTENT CREATION PROCESS

'I love having multiple spaces to talk to my community – I've learnt that cross-referencing content across different platforms can land very differently. Something I post on Instagram may not translate with my TikTok community, and my TikTok content may not land on the podcast. It's important to me to have multiple channels as it allows me to wear multiple hats.'

Amber Jeffrey, founder of
The Grief Gang podcast

If the idea of creating content makes you go into full meltdown mode, trust me: I see you. Having to constantly come up with new ideas and spin 10,000 additional plates at the same time can feel really tricky – I'm not denying that for one second. The task in itself can feel unbelievably mammoth. But I've learnt over time that having the right structure and foundations in place will make this process feel far smoother and – dare I say it – enjoyable! By implementing the steps that we're going to cover in this chapter – identifying your 'pillars'; developing a series; having a clear process; batching content; and analysing performance – you should have the knowledge and tools to bring your ideas to life with ease and find your content flow state.

BUILDING YOUR CONTENT ARCHITECTURE

When I was a kid, I'd beg my parents to let me stay up and watch *Grand Designs* (in case you're unfamiliar with *Grand Designs*, it's a British TV show that documents people building their dream homes). I loved seeing sketches of buildings come to life, the process of foundations being built and the home owners' personalities shining through.

Well, it turns out that building a content strategy and communicating who you are is much like my favourite nostalgic TV show and building a home. When you start to build a house, you work on the frame first, concrete is laid and the pillars go up so that it doesn't fall down. How you go on to communicate with your community has a very similar framework – here's why:

Your frame is your values, your purpose and your why. It's your selfhood. It's what props up the whole enterprise. Your pillars, aka content pillars, are what bring this to life. Content pillars are often called content buckets. However, I like to call them pillars simply because, when you visualise the infrastructure of a home, the frame and the pillars hold it up and keep it together. Your pillars are the key component to ensuring your content strategy is robust and stays standing for a long time.

Your content pillars should align with your values – they guide your messaging and talking points and help to ensure you're magnetising the right community.

I find that having my pillars mapped out is so helpful for when I'm ideating my content. I keep a notes section in my phone and on my laptop where I note down my pillars. Every time I have a new idea for a piece of content, or perhaps I see an article, I write the idea down or copy and paste the article into the relevant content pillar tab and refer back to it when I'm creating content. You may want to keep a notebook on you instead or use alternative software – it's entirely up to you how you choose to organise and document your content ideas.

When it comes to your pillars, you should aim to pick four to six 'themes' you want to talk about consistently throughout your content to prop up your business story and message. It's worth noting that your pillars may alternate, depending on the platforms you choose to use. For example, you may be speaking business-to-business over on LinkedIn, while your business-to-consumer community may live on other channels; therefore your topics may change (remember the margarita party from page 92). To show you what this could look like, I've outlined my own content pillars below:

1. Case studies: sharing examples of campaigns and content delivered by other businesses and providing commentary and take-aways on why it worked well, with insights for my community on how to apply the learnings to their own businesses.

2. Behind the scenes: sharing my process, how I approach projects, what I get up to in a day to offer a deeper, more personal approach to how I run The Selfhood.

3. Confidence: I know a huge pain point for my community is around confidently putting themselves out there and sharing their selfhood with the rest of the world. I often share confidence tips, advice and my personal story around confidence-boosting.

4. Marketing tips: sharing tips and tricks I've learnt through working with clients and building my community.

5. Mental health: I have collaborated with multiple mental-health charities to raise awareness of online well-being and protecting our energy and mental health in the online space. I often share advice and tips for protecting well-being online.

6. Sales: promoting my talks, services and products through my content.

At certain times of the year throughout your sales cycle you'll need to give greater weight to some pillars than others. Let's say you're a creator at the early stages of your journey and your focus is building your first 100 community members: you're going to need to focus on the pillars that showcase your personality so that people can really get to know you on a more personal level before committing to supporting your work and the rest of your journey.

If you're a product-based business and gifting periods are the time when your community typically buys from you most, you're going to want to focus on the pillars that best showcase your product's unique selling points and show them why it makes for such a great gift.

Your content strategy and therefore your pillars should always align with your overall business objectives (see page 32). Social media is not a separate entity to the rest of your business. I repeat: **social media is not a separate entity to the rest of your business**. What's happening online should reflect what's happening offline. If you have certain goals or objectives, then your social media channels should reflect that.

When considering your content pillars, it's important to refer back to the sweet spot exercise we did in Chapter 2, merging your values with your community's and working out how you can amplify and translate them into content pillars (see page 108). It's not uncommon for your values to overlap into pillars, so don't worry if your values are repeated here – this is often a good sign that your content is aligning with your overall purpose.

RINSE AND REPEAT

There's a common misconception that we can post about our product or service once and a thousand enquiries and sales will land in our laps immediately after. Sorry to break it to you: that is, in fact, wrong. Our worlds are filled with notifications. I might see a post while eating my yoghurt and save it or run for the bus and screen shot it with the intention of coming back to it, only to move on with my life and forget. It's a big ask to expect your community to remember your message, story or sales in one post. The general rule of thumb is as follows:

- It takes 5 views of a marketing message to read and digest it.
- It takes 10 views to become memorable.
- It takes 20 views for it to become a conversion.

So what does this mean for you? You need to get comfortable with repetition and also get creative with how you communicate and share your magic with your community. When I share that insight with people, the typical response I get is: 'Flippin' 'eck, everyone's going to be so bored of me!'

How about this fun fact for you: we're typically exposed to up to 10,000 marketing messages and ads *per day*.[1] You're up against 9,999 others trying to win over your community, and the only way to break through is by sharing your offer multiple times. If I asked you to reel off five social media posts that you saw yesterday, you probably wouldn't be able to. You might be able to give me two at a push. If you think that your community is going to remember every single post you ever put on your channels, then it's time to wake up and smell the cold, harsh scent of reality. You are not a pest, you are not annoying, you are not boring. Repetition is key for success.

Fashion consultant Elizabeth Stiles once shared that she had promoted her sell-out group programme over 200 times across her channels. That sounds like a lot, but it was done in such a way that it didn't feel repetitive or salesy. She wove in memes, videos, live Q&As, emails, collaborations, vlogs and behind-the-scenes content to keep the message varied.

I worked with Elizabeth to develop my first online workshop. When I showed her the promotional posts I'd created to sell my course, she flagged to me that I was just selling the deliverables and not the emotional benefit. She helped me work towards the 'what-you're-buying-versus-what-you're-getting' method:

What you're buying:

- A one-hour workshop
- 45 minutes of Q&A time
- An opportunity to network with like-minded business owners
- PDF worksheets to take away and fill in

What you're getting:

- Knowledge to last a lifetime
- 1:1 time with an expert
- The opportunity to expand your network and connect with new people
- A full document to refer back to and help you inform your business strategy

The last option is far more compelling, right? The values-and-benefits framework we went through in Chapter 2 (see page 102) can also help you build this technique when you're creating social media content and sales pages for your offers and products. I'd love for you to think about the benefits of what you do and what you offer beyond the physical deliverables: what will your community (and eventually your customers) gain from your product or service? Take out your notepad or type this up – you can always come back and build on it later.

CONTENT PROMPTS

Often businesses will reel off how great they are and list what they do, without thinking about how this could benefit or impact their community's lives. This often comes down to the language they use.

One of my favourite quotes to come back to when creating content is: 'You need to nuance how your brand manifests. It all starts with knowing your brand point of view and how you show up in culture' (Todd Kaplan, CMO of Pepsi).[2] I've worked with many businesses that have a completely different view of who they are versus what their community thinks of them because they're buried in details that, quite frankly, don't really matter and then they end up confused as to why their content isn't landing.

Often we're overcomplicating it, using jargon, trying to appear aspirational and distancing people in the process. You're competing for airtime among millions of other people, so it's important that your message is landing.

To help with this, I've listed a series of questions below for you to answer and start thinking about. You can also use your answers to fuel your captions and content. By doing this you will start to centre your community's experience with your product or service within your content as opposed to just telling them how great you are. The questions will prompt you into thinking about how your business plays a role in their lives on an emotive level.

- How does the work you do benefit your community?
- What are some of the scenarios you can describe where your community would need you?
- What problems do you solve?
- Are there any specific occasions where your product or service will be needed the most?
- How does what you do impact your community's lives?

STORY TIME
Many of the posts I've seen go viral and gain great traction with clients and other businesses have been about the business's story: the journey, how they got from A to B and the challenges faced along the way. This is what I like to think of as high-connectivity content as it shows your community what a journey it's been and helps build more of a human connection to the content you create. We're

naturally drawn to this content, and it's a great way to grow a closer bond with your audience. To help you with your own storytelling content, I've added some prompts to think about below:

- Why you chose the name for your business
- Your biggest challenge and how you overcame it
- Your very first prototype or service
- Your first ever piece of branding and how it evolved over time
- Your top five highlights so far and why
- A failure that was actually a blessing in disguise
- Something about running your business that used to terrify you, that you're now happy with
- Your proudest moment
- The moment that inspired you to start
- A series spotlighting different team members

REPURPOSING CONTENT

If the idea of content creation causes you to descend into creative block to the point where you start daydreaming about throwing in the towel and working on a remote micro-pig farm with no 5G and saying goodbye to the digital life, this section is for you.

Here is where you can stop planning your micro-pig getaway, because we're about to talk repurposing content. Repurposing content is what it says on the tin: it's about cross-pollinating certain content across your channels at different times. This concept is about to become your new best friend.

- Maximum impact: your community sees your message in multiple formats.
- Minimal thinking: you waste fewer brain calories having to ideate for all of the different channels.

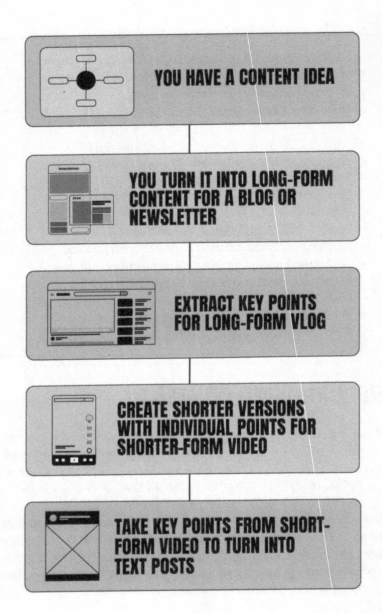

Now you can see how one idea can span across multiple channels. Not all of us have the same browsing behaviour: some like to read long form, some prefer video, others prefer snapshots and soundbites. By cross-pollinating your content, you cater to the different learning types in your community too.

Tip: when you're cross-pollinating content, ensure that your imagery and videos are created with the correct dimensions for each of the channels. Nowadays many of the apps will penalise you and lower the reach on your content if it is shared on their platforms with visible watermarks or native fonts from other apps (native fonts = fonts they provide you with when editing in the app). I would suggest you record the content outside of the apps and add any text within the individual apps to avoid any issues with your visibility. You don't need fancy editing software – there are many free and easy-to-use apps such as *InShot* which you can use to edit your content to a high standard.

CREATING A CONTENT SERIES

As humans, we're drawn to reinforcement which is why we love TV series and, in more recent years, podcasts. Dr Renee Carr, a clinical psychologist, says, '[Dopamine] gives the body a natural, internal reward of pleasure that reinforces continued engagement in that activity. It's the brain's signal that communicates to the body – this feels good. You should keep doing this!'[3]

Our brains quite literally tell us to keep watching series for a few different reasons:

- Consistent set-up: we seek comfort in familiarity and the repetition of the series.
- Character investment: we become attached to characters and people the more we see them.
- Consistent storytelling: storytelling is a vital part of our human functioning. It elicits learnings, entertainment and emotional attachments.

My first ever content series was called 'Advice that changed my life'. I created over 20 TikTok videos sharing different pieces of advice that went on to change my life, all of them linked back to my overall business message and my thoughts on confidence and showing up in your business as your true self. I saw my biggest spike in community engagement when I posted this series, and cross-pollinated the content across my newsletter, LinkedIn and Instagram channels to get the most out of it.

My community went on to stitch some of the videos (stitching = where someone reposts your video with their own next to it, usually accompanied with a commentary or text) and shared their own life advice, which created a ripple effect of wholesome advice across TikTok.

A series will also help you dig deep into topics. Often we're victims of feeling as though our knowledge is 'basic' because we eat, sleep and breathe it, so it becomes second nature. You have to remember that often the things that feel glaringly obvious to you are gold dust to someone else. Whenever I host my community Q&As and workshops, I am reminded of this – don't ever assume your community knows everything.

Tip: write down all of the subjects that you could go on to create a series from. Don't worry about this feeling too 'basic'. I often see social media posts packed with amazing content; however, they feel overwhelming because there's too much to digest. Sometimes bite-sized content works better, particularly with a series.

POINTERS FOR PLANNING YOUR CONTENT
The famous saying goes, 'If you fail to plan, you plan to fail' and this rings particularly true with content. You could have the most original, engaging and disruptive content ideas going, but without any thought on how you're going to achieve them, the only place they're going to land is in your head.

- Have a central document that you work from: this could be a spreadsheet or alternative piece of software to plan your posts in. It's important that you stick to this to help you stay on track and strategically plan your content in advance.
- Refer back to your content pillars to get inspired and help you elevate your story. Remember that your pillars act as your content architecture and will guide you in creating content that is relevant to your audience. Reference each pillar within your plan so that you can see how much you are talking about each specific pillar.
- Try to plan at least one week in advance: this will give you the opportunity to be reactive and think about the bigger picture. Some people plan more than one week in advance – there is no right or wrong here. However, having a plan is important as this will give you headspace to create 'reactive content'. Reactive content is content that you can create when something is trending in your industry or when you need to tap into culturally relevant moments.
- Dedicate time in your calendar to work on content creation so that you can build it in as a habit: find a time in your weekly or monthly schedule that works best for you and get batching! I'll be honest, this requires discipline and you may not always stick to the same day . . . However, having a routine in place will help you get into a creative cycle and give your content the time and energy it deserves.

I have created a free content-calendar download in the resources hub that you can use to strategically plan your own content. I would highly recommend that you use this as it will help you get organised and look at your content plans with more thought and structure. When you start to work on your content calendar, you should put your content purpose in there (see page 99). This will encourage you to really think about the why behind your online content, and, ultimately, keep your community front of mind before you hit the post button.

BEHIND-THE-SCENES CONTENT

A short while ago, I was hosting a social media strategy workshop for a business with well over 1 million followers on social media. It has lots of people following its journey and, at the time, the business was doing well, but it wanted to work on a community-engagement strategy and nurture its relationships with its biggest advocates.

It was (and still is) a very creative brand with a strong aesthetic that has been years in the making. It is idolised by competitors for its innovations and some of its community even have its designs tattooed on them.

We worked on revamping the brand's strategy from purely editorial and campaign product-focused glossy imagery to sharing the behind the scenes – the creative process and content that showcased the creativity of the team in an on-brand way which felt aligned to its aesthetic and values without compromising the premium feel of its work.

We saw that the content that spotlighted the internal process and teams had nearly triple the engagement rate. The juicy stuff that showcased what went on inside the four walls of ideation sessions and a day in the life of the team, the videos that showcased the colourful and stylised prints on the exposed office brick work, the array of coffee orders spanning from creamy oat milk lattes to black Americanos ordered from the local coffee shop in creative ideation sessions, the blow-up neon bubble chairs scattered in the break-out areas in the office, the old-school vintage memorabilia from previous collections that sat archived around the space and the grainy, raw, behind-the-scenes video content from street-styled looks they'd captured on shoots – it blew up. The engagement sky-rocketed and so did the influx of followers and subscribers.

While this content didn't drive a huge amount of click-throughs and traffic initially, it grew the brand's awareness and following on its channels and, after a few months, we saw that the social to website traffic increased significantly and this also converted into sales. We also saw that community interactions and news-letter sign-ups grew in tandem.

When I've shared this case study previously, I've had pushback that behind-the-scenes content will devalue a brand. At this point I usually pull up fashion magazine *Vogue*'s YouTube chan-nel and unpack their behind-the-scenes content.

Vogue, like many other premium and luxury brands, shares behind-the-scenes content – the kind that provides context to elaborate campaigns and big collaborations. It gives us a window into the creative process and a deeper admiration for the work and execution. It's still shot beautifully and has an aspirational feel; however, it gives us a deeper connection to the work. So if your concern is that your behind-the-scenes content is going to devalue your brand, rest assured that you can still execute it in an aspirational way.

You see, the behind the scenes of your business doesn't necessarily mean videos of you in your dressing gown on a Monday morning after a weekend on the spicy margaritas or the questionable-looking attempt at the viral mac and cheese you saw on TikTok and made your partner for dinner. Depending on the nature of your busi-ness and your community values, what you choose to share is entirely up to you. A lot of premium and luxury brands now share their creative process and even their supply-chain systems for extra transparency as they know that their communities value seeing the full picture when it comes to their business. Equally, if you don't feel comfortable doing that, that's also totally fine.

Behind-the-scenes content is not only effective for showcasing how your offer works, it also furthers the value. You don't have to spill all of your secret sauce or share the bespoke method-ologies behind what you do, particularly if you have patented products or a one-of-a-kind workflow that you don't want to share. It's about conveying your unique story, which is paramount to showcasing your selfhood.

Tip: document everything – I mean everything. Create a folder of images and videos and use it as a back-up for the days you don't have content captured. It's better to capture more than you think you need as you never know when the extra content will come in handy. Remember, you can also repurpose your content which we'll get to on page 129.

'PEOPLE BUY FROM PEOPLE'

This phrase pains me, but it's true. We are drawn to people by nature; it's why brands pay creators, influencers and celebrities to endorse their products because they know that people are more likely to buy from a human than a brand with a transaction in mind. Before we break this down, I'm going to explain the difference between influencers and creators as they often get mistaken for one another:

Influencers: do what they say on the tin: influence. Often have their own communities and work with brands to promote their products in the hopes of increased brand awareness and sales for the brand. This is often their full-time job and they generate revenue by promoting brands' products with paid-for promotions and affiliate links.

Creators: often have jobs outside of creating content and work with brands to create content as a side hustle. This content is often used for the brand's organic channels and isn't always posted on the creators' profiles as it's more often than not for brand purposes. This type of content is also referred to as user generated content aka 'UGC'. Due to the creator economy, we are seeing more full-time creators emerge.

The behind-the-scenes content translating to community-engagement theory comes to life when we look at influencers and creators who birth their own businesses. In recent years, the creator economy has boomed. HubSpot recorded that, as of 2022, the creator economy market size was estimated at $104.2 billion – more than double its value since 2019.[4] This is only set to grow dramatically as shiny and forced-upon-us narratives shift to real stories. Many brands such as Gymshark and LVMH have gone on to recruit influencers and celebrities as creative directors as they know that influencers understand how to grow loyal and engaged communities.

As a result, many influencers and creators have gone on to start their own businesses ranging from fitness apps, beauty brands, clothing lines and more. A common thread we see is that the posts on the influencers' and creators' social media profiles will receive much higher engagement than the posts we see on their business profiles promoting a product. Why? Because we've been taken on their journies. We know what their families, friends and partners are like. We've seen them go through highs, lows, break-ups, transformations and a whole lot more, so we connect with them more naturally.

I don't share this to encourage you to talk about the barney that you had with your partner because they ate your leftover pizza – you don't have to go that far. This is merely food for thought (excuse the terrible pun) as to how powerful behind-the-scenes and high-connectivity content really is. A human approach will always win – that's why brands now invest so much in collabo-rating with influencers, creators and niche communities. They know the landscape has changed and consumers buy into people, and people birth real and meaningful tribes. We're going to cover this in more detail in the next chapter.

CREATE INTIMATE SPACES

A few years ago I was on my way to a meeting when my Instagram and Facebook pages completely stopped working. I thought it was my signal readjusting after getting off the Tube, but I soon realised this wasn't just a 'me problem'. I headed to Twitter and it became clear at that point that the Meta-owned channels were completely down. No feeds were refreshing whatsoever – the media coined it 'the blackout'.

Among the stressed Mark Zuckerberg memes and multiple threads, lay another theme: sheer panic. I was one of those panicked people. I started thinking about my clients and how they had become so reliant on their social media communities. I started thinking about my own community and how I'd prioritised social media for so long and started to catastrophise about how I'd find new business without any awareness at all.

That was a big wake-up call for me and, from that moment, I committed to building out more intimate spaces for myself and for clients, so that we could reach our communities without having to rely on third-party platforms to act as go-betweens. Aside from sleeping at night without the fear of the likes of Zuckerbergs and Musks wiping out community hubs altogether, there are also a multitude of other benefits that come with having intimate spaces for your communities to connect.

Social media users have become wiser in understanding how their data is being used, and many tech companies have come under fire regarding their advertising standards. As a result, Apple introduced in-app tracking (this is where users are prompted to agree to tracking or opt out when downloading a new app, including social media apps) and Google is working on phasing out third-party cookies (cookies = the tracking on a website that remembers your info; it's how Amazon knows your language, where you live and your obscene coffee-pod addiction when you log in). What does that mean for you? Advertising and tracking are essentially a lot harder these days – the ability to attain a high degree of visibility through ads will decrease, which means that having organic and intimate spaces we can connect with our communities in will be super important.

The Diary Of A CEO is a weekly podcast series hosted by Steven Bartlett. He interviews guests about the highs and lows of their careers and uncovers their personal stories. The podcast has a community of millions spanning from YouTube, Instagram and TikTok to Telegram. Steven has strategically created a space for intimate updates where he shares voice notes with his community which feel personal, like a close friend checking in. He offers sneak peaks and early access to merchandise and products. He encourages conversations through the use of polls and quizzes and is vulnerable about the ups and downs of the podcast.

This is a clever technique because a) his highly engaged community gets one-on-one access to him and other members in an intimate space that feels personal and b) he's created a space to talk to his community outside of traditional apps.

> 'Our Telegram community is significantly smaller than our core social media communities. We have around 28k followers there and we have millions elsewhere. But they are by far our most loyal and engaged – they're our brand ambassadors. We can ask them questions, trial things, they're real people, they're our live focus group. They're the first channel we consult and go to when it comes to testing new products or concepts. People try to create these intimate communities and they fail because they ask more than they're giving. Offer them intimate access that you can't get elsewhere.'

> **Grace Andrews, head of social media and content, *The Diary Of A CEO***

Fashion brand All Saints has a Discord channel where it shares sneak peaks of new collections and asks its community to provide feedback. It hosts live Q&As with product designers where its community can ask questions about the products, and it has a dedicated community manager who moderates the channel and encourages conversations.

Before you start growing an intimate space though, there are a few things to consider:

DO YOU HAVE TIME?
Be realistic here. Intimate spaces require upkeep – you need to engage your community and check in with them often to enable conversation and keep the chat alive.

IS THERE A DEMAND FOR IT?
Does your community really want this? Qualify the need first by asking them about their preferred channel. For example, a business-to-business may use Slack over WhatsApp as many people prefer to keep their personal and business conversations separate. Business-to-consumer may look at using Discord or WhatsApp (depending on where your community hangs out most).

As with everything we've discussed so far, make sure that you're researching first and, if you have a community already, get their feedback and talk to them to understand where and how they'd like to hear from you.

CAN YOU SAFEGUARD?
Are you on hand to look out for any trolls or negativity? What's your strategy and approach if these become an issue (see page 230 for more on dealing with trolls)? Don't wait for a situation to arise – ensure you have an agreed plan for any crisis that happens so that you're ready to press play on your response quickly.

WHAT'S THE INCENTIVE?
Make sure you're clear on the offer and the why for your community to take the next step into migrating onto your safe space. Can you take a learning from Steven Bartlett and give them more personal updates, 1:1 time and Q&As? What is the reward for the community?

YOUR CONTENT ISN'T BORING

When we see 'likes' and engagement on our posts, this prompts our brains into releasing dopamine. As a result, we deem content that doesn't receive lots of engagement as 'shit content' and end up thinking that we're really boring and everyone hates us. This isn't the case – your brain is tricking you and no one hates you.

MAKE IT EVERGREEN

We have to remember that our social media profiles act as our portfolios. The post may not resonate with your community there and then, but someone may find you, fall in a content rabbit hole and find that old post and it could resonate at a later date. I have videos on my Selfhood channels that are months and often years old that people reference when they enquire with me or come to my events. Community-serving content isn't just about gratification in the moment of posting – it's about creating evergreen content that can be referenced later on.

Here are two examples:

Jacob is a graphic designer. He posts a behind-the-scenes tutorial for a fancy poster he made for a passion project and it gets lots of views and engagement. The post performs well in the algorithms, Jacob gains some new followers and the new community members who came in from the high-performing post convert into sales further down the line.

Cool, so the post served its purpose in attracting new people. Jacob could post about his services and how to work with him. One week later and the post receives low engagement. Jacob becomes deflated and starts to doubt his popularity within his community.

Let's backtrack for a second: not everyone in Jacob's community is ready to commit yet – they need to be nurtured and wined and dined first. Therefore, the promotional content isn't relevant to them right now. However, the new community members who stumble across Jacob's work via the poster video may find that content at a later date and make an enquiry.

Charlie is a DIY homeware brand owner. She makes bespoke glassware, mugs and vases for people's homes. Charlie shares an interior-design video featuring her products and it blows up. She gains thousands of new followers and her community grows.

Charlie then goes on to share that she now makes bespoke birthday gifts too. The post doesn't perform so well and Charlie considers moving to Easter Island and throwing her phone in the sea for good.

Let's rewind. Charlie's community who flew in from the interior-design post then start to see more of her posts in the feed, they like and engage and then one day decide to take a deeper look at her content. It's their mum's birthday next week and guess what? She loves a vase.

You see the point? **A flop isn't always a flop.** This is a really important message for you to think about, especially when you're promoting to your community. Most of the time your promotional content will perform worse than your brand content because not everyone is ready to commit to a purchase or conversion yet. Therefore the content doesn't speak to them directly at that time. This is where planning comes in and you can begin to increase the volume of your promotional content to create an effective pre-launch strategy for your community.

DUST YOURSELF OFF AND TRY AGAIN

I once created a video about how to speak more confidently on camera. I mapped out a script and spent hours editing the video and the engagement was terrible. I'll be honest, I was so embarrassed, which was ironic because it was a video about confronting your speaking fears and confidence, and there I was feeling deflated that no one had 'liked' my efforts.

It was strange to me because I knew that this was a topic that my community asked about often, and it always came up during my webinars and focus groups. I took the key points from the post and put it into a long-form newsletter and packaged the information into a carousel post on Instagram. The newsletter went on to be one of my most opened and clicked emails and the carousel post had great engagement and led to a booking for a corporate-speaking gig. Wanting to test my theory further, I created a video using the same information and packaged it up into shorter-form version with a more compelling opening line which performed far better.

The lesson here: **sometimes it's not about the topic or the content itself, it's about the execution**. It could be that the video doesn't land in the first three seconds (which is the time it takes someone to decide whether they're going to continue watching); it could be that you posted it at the wrong time of day (see below for more on this); it could be that the post was too wordy or the sound was off. There are a multitude of reasons as to why posts 'flop' sometimes.

If you have a great concept, keep trying. Equally, if you have a great concept, repurpose it. No one is going to remember what you posted about six months ago and call you out for repurposing a great message. If they do, they need to get a hobby. This will also help drive forward your rinse-and-repeat method (see page 111) and hammer your message home.

At the end of each quarter, I check my social media insights and do a recap on what performed well and repurpose it into a new format or change the messaging slightly. I once had a fashion-brand client who consistently saw that mirror selfies featuring their product drove sales. We identified this pattern and briefed our content creators to take mirror selfies to continue to repurpose this method. Until you repurpose and switch up the creative output or messaging slightly, you just won't know. The important thing to remember is that if your engagement is low on a particular piece of content, it doesn't mean that it's a pile of shit and you should move to Easter Island with Charlie.

WHEN YOU SHOULD POST

Although time of day isn't the be-all and end-all of your posting strategy, this doesn't mean to say that you should post any time of day and hope for the best. It's important to consider the mindset of your community before you post. For example, my insights tell me my community is most active after 6pm, however my posts perform better in the morning or at lunchtime, as I'm often sharing business-related questions and my community are less engaged with business chat post 6pm when they've logged off and are unwinding from work. Many of my e-commerce clients see success in the evenings and on Sundays as their communities are in post-work mode, are browsing more leisurely and ready to commit to buying. Your analytics (see below) can help you understand buying and engagement patterns. This information will come in particularly useful for launches, and can help you determine your email marketing times too.

DEALING WITH TRAFFIC TUMBLEWEED

A common pattern I see when looking at sign-ups and sales cycles is that there's a huge spike on launch day (providing you've worked on a pre-launch hype strategy), then typically a flat line with a few anomalies in between and a big spike when the 'last-chance-to-buy'/'stock is low, grab-it-now' messaging comes in. This is where traffic tumbleweed occurs.

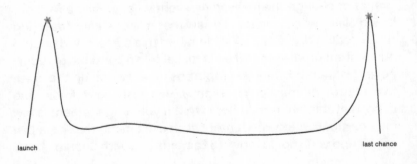

launch   last chance

'Traffic tumbleweed' is a phrase I coined a few years ago after noticing a phenomenon of slow sales in between announcement date and last-chance-to-buy in the sales cycle. It happens to people selling courses, digital products, new collections and tickets to events. This is totally normal and a very common pattern. You can't let this put you off selling and drive you to posting paralysis (feeling totally and utterly overwhelmed to the point where you shut down your laptop, ghost your phone, abort the idea altogether and then panic that you haven't posted and repeat the cycle).

I want to acknowledge this now because you need to get comfortable with the fact that your traction may slow down. That is normal, and it's OK. Whenever I promote a new product or service, I see my highest sign-ups come in the day I close the doors because often people need to be prompted and reminded that it's their last chance – because people are busy. It can sometimes go the other way around: an influx of sales on launch day and hearing nothing but crickets after.

This is where you rinse and repeat (see page 111): sell through the silence; repeat your story and your message; and keep getting creative. You may wallow so hard you dive head-first into a cringe attack, but that's OK. Remember what I said about the thousands of social media posts per day? If you think John is going to remember that you promoted your new collection or programme at precisely 11am on Monday and can recite your caption word for word, then it's time to get out of your head, immediately.

It's also worth noting that launches and promoting your new products and services is a great way to experiment with your messaging and analyse what's working. **Nothing is ever a flop – there is always insight in the lessons.** You can then start to get analytical about what worked and what didn't work: did a particular channel perform really well and another not so much? Did a particular post resonate more than others?

THE POWER OF ANALYSIS

Many businesses come to me because they're stuck in a rut with their communities. Often their communities have tapped out from engaging, stopped buying or their behavioural habits have changed. Sometimes the business saw a spike in sales and they died off and they can't figure out why. The first thing I ask is, 'Have you run an audit and checked your analytics?' The response is more often than not, 'Erm, no'.

To me, analytics are the free gold dust that so many business owners and social media managers sit on; I am always flabbergasted to learn that people aren't utilising the power of analysis. A client of mine once described analytics as 'Kind of like maths GCSE – definitely necessary but not as fun as art'. Sure, creating content, filming campaigns, coming up with the big-thinking stuff is more sexy and fun, but without knowledge of what is fuelling your business, how can you pull together strategic ideas? Without understanding the ecosystem of how your content feeds into your other channels, what content drives engagement, what content leads to click-through and who is actually engaging with you, you're essentially ideating out of thin air and hoping for the best.

Whenever I work with a new client or take on a new project, the first thing I do is conduct an audit so that I can see what's really going on. Most of the time there are lots of gems hiding in the analysis; some are obvious and others take a little digging, but without the reporting and the deep dive they're hard to uncover.

INCREASING REVENUE ONE HANDBAG AT A TIME

Before I founded The Selfhood I worked in the digital marketing team at the global fashion and accessories brand Skinnydip London. Skinnydip sells a variety of products spanning from clothing, accessories, beauty products and more, but it's known best for its phone cases which have been seen on celebrities such as Kylie Jenner. When I joined the company, its customer profiles were strictly 16–24-year-old women in the UK. It wasn't advertising to any other demographics and its organic social media channels reflected this too – the tone of voice was very young and the content had a Gen Z aesthetic.

During my first week at the company, I was asked to pull an analytics report. I looked at the website traffic, sales data, email marketing, paid advertising and organic social media statistics. What I found was that the younger social media demographic were coming to the website, buying products with a low transaction value and coming back at a later date to buy again. I also found that women over the age of 25 in the UK and US were coming to the website, spending triple on their first transaction and coming back at a later date and spending considerably more than the younger demographic. I took this insight to the founders and we began running paid social adverts to this audience and saw a 30 per cent uplift in revenue within a matter of months.

Had we not run an analytics report we wouldn't have known about the two additional captive audiences. We were able to then create unique email marketing segments for this new-found demographic and nurture them into a community. Using the data from the products they were buying, we were able to serve them different content to the content we had historically been blanket serving. The design team went on to create more 'mature' products as we expanded the personas, and even went on to open stores in the US based on our online sales and traffic data.

Running analytics reports isn't just about monitoring your growth, it's about identifying areas to grow and expand on. It's about finding opportunities and leaning into them. The Skinnydip example is one of many nuggets of wisdom I've come to find when running analytics reports for businesses. Most social media scheduling tools offer detailed analytics information, and the social media platforms themselves mostly offer in-app analytics too.

As well as checking your social media analytics, it's important to gauge how your website traffic is impacted by your social media content too. Many website providers will offer analytics reports for you. However, Google Analytics is a free tool that you can use which will give you detailed reports showing you your website demographics and the main websites that are referring website traffic to you (for example, press links, blog posts, social media sites and affiliate sites if you work with them). This information can help you understand what channels are driving traffic and conversions so you can start to explore your options more heavily as you begin to understand the different channels that your community is coming from.

METRICS WORTH MENTIONING

It's important to understand that social media is not just a marketing tool – it's not about posting to purely drive sales and revenue. It's part of a much bigger journey, and we're going to talk about this community journey in Chapter 7; however, I want you to start thinking about the metrics that are important beyond just revenue and likes.

Engagement rate

Most industries have a different average engagement rate, so it's worth doing some research into the average engagement rate for your industry and understanding where you sit within this.

Growth rate

As we've already discussed, followers and subscribers are not the be-all and end-all of a strong community. However, growing is a sign that your existing community is advocating for you and that your content is reaching the right people.

It's important to caveat here that, often, people aspire for 'virality'. Viral videos can be great, but they can also be damaging. I've seen people go viral and bring in a huge influx of followers who don't need or want what the business is offering. They then stop engaging with future content, which goes on to affect the brand's overall engagement rate and the business then suffers. Of course, there can be many positives to going viral too. But ultimately, when you're thinking about going viral it's important to ensure all content is in line with the content pillars we discussed in Chapter 5 and the brand values you established in Chapter 2.

Percentage of video viewed

If you're creating video content, it's good to get into the habit of checking what percentage of your video is being watched to gauge any drop-offs. It might be that you need to work on keeping your community engaged. I'd suggest you create a 'hook' for your video to spark intrigue and entice viewers to keep watching. Keep storytelling throughout with visuals and voice-overs.

Due to the rise of platforms such as TikTok, many people believe that long-form content is over – it's absolutely not. YouTube is still a key player in the content mix and there is a huge appetite for longer-form content. TikTok now allows for longer-form content, as does Pinterest. This is where you can think strategically about repurposing content (see page 115).

Shares

Due to privacy settings, some channels won't allow you to see how many shares your posts have had, while others will. This is a good indicator of the content that your community is finding useful or entertaining and sharing with their peers.

Saves

This is a great indicator that the content you've shared holds so much value that people want to return to it. It's worth keeping an eye on any patterns in the content that gets saved so that you can do more of the same.

Positive comments

This is a great signal that your community is interacting with your content and taking the extra step to spark conversation. When it comes to community-building in particular, positive comments are one of the key signals that your content is serving its purpose and starting conversations and interactions (aka building and growing connections).

Website clicks

Having an understanding of the types of content that are navigating people outside of the apps and onto your website/alternative platforms is a great measure of how your content is converting and how effective your calls to action are.

It's also worth bearing in mind that, depending on your goals, some of these metrics will be more important than others. For example, if you're a new business, your goal will most likely be brand awareness and growth to aid you in securing your first 100 customers. Therefore, your growth metrics will be key at this stage. If you're an established business looking to generate sales, you will want to focus on your website clicks and social traffic to see how well your content is performing. We're going to take a deep dive into the community journey and the content that performs well at the different stages of the community life cycle in the next chapter.

In the resources hub I've created a template analytics report that you can use for your own social media accounts to use and report on, on a monthly basis.

Process, planning and analysing your content performance isn't the most 'fun' part of growing a community, especially if you're creative and find structure challenging (I feel you, by the way). However, I really want to reaffirm the importance of all of these components. Without a process you can't create a plan; without a plan your content won't have any thought or strategy behind it; and without analysing what's working how can you capitalise on your learnings and keep serving your community with the content they enjoy seeing from you? This will set you up for success and help you find your creative flow. Consider this the groundwork for creating an amazing online experience and journey for your community. With the groundwork in place you can make informed decisions about how to look at your channels holistically.

THE FUTURE OF CONTENT CREATION

At the time of writing this book many developments are happening in the artificial intelligence (AI) space (and at rapid speed). Software such as Chat GPT (a website that writes content copy for you with input and guidance from you as the user) and auto generated text to image software such as Adobe Firefly, have been adopted as part of the content process at record breaking speed. I want to say that while yes, AI is worth exploring and implementing as part of your process to help you save time creating and give you more time to innovate and work on the bigger picture. It is worth noting that nothing will ever replace real human storytelling and your own lived experience. I would urge you to not become too reliant on AI and dig deep into your own story as we've been through within the book, as your own story can never be replaced.

CHAPTER RECAP

- Establish your content pillars: get clear on your four to six themes and start to build content ideas around this.
- Start a content bank folder and document everything. Even the 'boring' stuff.
- Research the different intimate spaces you could bring your community to further down the line. Think about your incentive and the why behind the space: what is the value for them joining? How are you going to facilitate this in a way that accommodates your schedule and capacity without burning out?
- Monitor your efforts and utilise your data. They can fuel wider business decisions, present huge opportunities and help you understand your community on a more granular level.

Chapter 7

WORK ON YOUR COMMUNITY JOURNEY

'Having clear communication and constant feedback is important – at the beginning, we grew so fast so self-evaluation was hard to do. We now do a yearly end-of-year reflection together and look at what we want to change and what we do well. We're a lot more open now/transparent with each other within the collective.'

Nadī – Samia, DJ, creative producer and broadcaster

I often say that building a community is like dating – you have to wine and dine your community before you expect them to buy into you. There's a whole process that needs to happen before they commit to you and, in this chapter, I'll tell you exactly how to create and nurture an effective community journey.

BIG GROUPIE ENERGY

The year was 2006. I was 14, and my bi-monthly music genre of choice was emo rock. I had a swoop fringe that dominated the majority of the right side of my face, pinned down erratically with brightly coloured hair clips. I wore fingerless gloves, thick black eyeliner and band T-shirts that had skulls all over them. Much to my mum's annoyance, the aesthetic I had adopted had a loud and turbulent playlist to match.

Like most hormonal teenagers, I had posters of my favourite musicians on my wall and would stare at them longingly after school, praying for the day I would eventually go on to marry them and birth their children.

One day, a notification popped up on the nostalgic music plat-form – Myspace, alerting me that one of my favourite bands at the time was playing at the 02 Academy in Brixton, south London. I remember physically shaking at the prospect of meeting my favourite band and future husband(s). Within two minutes I was on the phone to my best friend: 'OH MY GOD, TBS ARE PLAYING IN BRIXTON!' I screamed. After we'd recovered from our meltdowns and begged our mums to buy us tickets, I spent the next three months planning my wedding outfit.

When the day came and my favourite band emerged on stage, I was in love. Starstruck. A total mess. I think I cried the entire time, coyly and intermittently wiping my tears between songs in case they noticed me and wanted to propose to me in front of everyone. The gig ended and it riddles my entire body with cringe now, but we waited outside the stage door for the band for an hour.

When the lead singer made his way out – and to this day I can't explain to you how or why I did this – I half-screamed, half-cried, 'ADAM, I LOVE YOU!' The rest of the band all proceeded to laugh and, bizarrely, he didn't propose to me there and then.

That night, I went home, reflected on my choices and a part of my soul died. You'll be pleased to know that I vowed to myself I would never declare my love to a stranger ever again.

You might be thinking what's my weird PDA got to do with your community-building strategy? Well, the same rules apply for you when you're asking your community to join you on your journey and eventually buy from you and stay loyal. It's your job to wine and dine them; otherwise, you're going to get pied like I did.

THE LIFE CYCLE OF A COMMUNITY

Before we dig into creating your digital journey, it's important that you understand your community life cycle as you'll need to consider this before you start to map out your marketing ecosystem. As your community grows and you attract new fans, you're going to have a bunch of people who are all at different stages in their journey with you. For some you are only just on their radar, while others will have been with you from the beginning. It's important to recognise this so that your messaging, calls to action and content cater to your different community stages.

Think of it this way: you wouldn't walk up to someone you've never met in your local supermarket and say, 'Holy bananas, you're incredible. Wanna come back to mine?' (I mean, if you would, hats off to you. I'm intrigued to know your conversion rate.)

STAGE 1: LINGERING LINDAS (AKA THE OBSERVERS)

This person is lingering in the shadows. Their friends have sent them your content, their colleague was praising you at the team bonding night and their mother-in-law swears by you. They've heard your name through their own contacts and they're curious. After a while, they hit the 'follow' or 'subscribe' button and start to observe you.

They suss out if you're their vibe or not. If they like what they see, they take the next step and evolve into a 'Clapping Collin' (see below).

Tip: a reintroduction post every few months is a really great way to remind people who you are, what you do and how you can help/what you offer. This is something I do personally, and I often get enquiries (even from people who have been following for a while) after I reintroduce myself on my social media channels.

STAGE 2: CLAPPING COLLINS (CHEERING YOU ON FROM AFAR)

This group of people are interested in you, but they're not quite 'in the club' yet; there's still some work to do here. They've been following your journey for a little while – they may engage with your content, they may start to leave comments and show interest in the work that you do, but they're not talking to your key community and advocates yet; they're not quite in the official squad.

When trying to magnetise this group of people, it's important to remember this interaction is a two-way street. If someone is taking time and effort to engage with you, it's your job to engage back. If you owned a physical shop or space and someone walked in and complimented your work or products and you totally ignored them they'd think you were rude and leave to go to your competitor. The same goes for online exchanges: if someone is taking their time to interact with you, use this as a time to acknowledge or engage.

Tip: allocate time within your week to focus on responding to comments and messages. Depending on the size and scale of your business and the number of interactions you have, you may want to look at recruiting a full- or part-time community manager or look at a community-management tool to help you manage the influx of messages and requests you get. Do not ignore these people – they are one step on the ladder to becoming your superfans.

STAGE 3: MEGAPHONE MANDYS (ADVOCATES FOR YOU BEHIND THE SCENES)

Megaphone Mandys don't just engage with you, they tell their friends, colleagues and anyone who will listen about you. You're their crush and they're not even afraid to show it: they've gone public with it. They share your posts in WhatsApp groups and to their own feeds, and advocate for you when they're out for a mid-week catch up.

They've probably bought from you a good few times, but they're not 100 per cent loyal. Mandys like to play the field a little and flirt with your competitors, so there is still a little work to be done in getting them to become #official with you.

Tip: this is when you can start to incentivise them to get jiggy with you. Can you migrate them to an additional channel, like your newsletter, and wine and dine them there? Can you get them to attend an event, workshop or join a more intimate space, such as a webinar or Discord channel?

STAGE 4: DIEHARD DENNISES (GROUPIE MATERIAL; FOLLOWS YOUR EVERY MOVE AND WOULD RUN TO THE END OF THE EARTH FOR YOU)

Goodness me, Diehard Dennis is obsessed with you and not even afraid to show it - it's a PDA showdown. Dennis sets an alarm when you announce that something is newly available to buy or engage with so that they can be the first to try it.

Dennis wants everyone to know about your relationship - they interact with fellow Dennises, share your work, proactively tell you how great you are and continue to buy from you and engage with you.

Tip: don't get complacent: Dennises know they need to be treated like royalty and they're not afraid to find a better option if you start to go cold on them.

STAGE 5: OG OLGAS (YOUR DAY ONES)

Ah, Olga, from the good ol' days. OG Olgas have been with you since day one. They've been here from the get-go and stuck around to support your success - they're your advocates. They transitioned all the way through from Lindas and have been on the journey with you since the beginning. Olgas are happy to see you thrive, continuously clap for you, participate in everything you do and buy from you consistently.

Olgas have put a ring on it - you're official. They'll always come back to you and certainly don't have a wandering eye. They do, however, expect to love and be loved in return and, while they're very patient with you while you wine and dine your Lindas, Collins, Mandys and Dennises, they do expect the utmost TLC - and, if we're being honest, they deserve it.

Tip: make your Olgas feel like the VIPs that they are. You may create a special segment on your newsletter list and give them first access to your offers and incentives; you may surprise them with discounts, introduce a loyalty scheme , VIP events, or reward them in a way that feels good for you (more on this later).

TAKE CARE OF THEM

It's important to remember this: **the cost of acquiring a new customer or community member is more expensive than retaining an old one.** When you factor in the time, energy and effort of marketing and overheads, it's still lucrative for you to be re-engaging your loyal customers. Of course, growth is a key metric for most businesses and you should absolutely be looking at acquiring new community members who will eventually convert into customers, but, at the same time, you need to acknowledge the ones who have remained loyal from the beginning.

I say this because, when building a brand or business online, people are often blind-sided by vanity metrics, such as followers, subscribers and fans. I can assure you now, as someone who has worked with global brands, start-ups and everyone else in between, that you can still have a very successful brand without a huge following.

Your following, community and eventually customers are more than just a number. They will be magnetised to you for your values, how you communicate and the attentive care you show your existing community. That is how you grow and evolve sustainably. Sure, there are some 'growth hacks' you can apply to your business, and you may see a short-term spike in growth when it comes to subscribers and follows, but if you're not transitioning your Lindas to your Dennises, your growth will flatline and your business will become redundant very quickly.

No one really owes it to you to stay loyal. There are lots of people out there and the competition is high, which is why you need to work on becoming irreplaceable and making them feel valued.

Now we've been through the life cycle, it's important that you understand the ways in which you can transition your Lindas into becoming Dennises through the different marketing channels.

START FLIRTING AND BUILDING YOUR FUNNEL

There is a wine-and-dine process that needs to happen before you can ask people to buy into what you do. The same way we have to work on our relationships, we have to work on our audience and convert them over to join our communities. We've established the attributes of your Lingering Lindas, Clapping Collins, Megaphone Mandys, Diehard Dennises and OG Olgas. Now we need to establish the process we take them through to migrate them from Lindas to Dennises. This is where your 'funnel' comes in.

I personally dislike the word 'funnel' – it feels kinda sterile and jargony to me when, in reality, your funnel is a beautiful process of nourishing the relationship between you and your community. As we work through this chapter, I would like for you to think of your 'funnel' as a community journey. This is how I prefer to refer to it as really that is what a funnel is, a journey in to your world and the story you tell along the way. As with your business story, your unique values and ethos, your community journey will be different to others, based on how you plan to serenade them.

Despite the fact that your community journey will be different to mine, and mine will be different to someone else's, its structure should always be laid out in the phases that follow, as this will help you strategically plan your content and work in a flow and cycle for your community:

- Top of funnel: this is typically the research phase for your community and often their first encounter with you or your brand. Top-of-funnel methods are often achieved with out-of-home advertising such as billboards and public-transport ads, PR, influencer partnerships, collaborations, paid social media ads, video content or, my personal favourite, word-of-mouth or recommendation. Essentially, it's the place people may stumble across you. This is where your Lingering Lindas are hiding.

- Middle of funnel: this is where your community takes the next step – they may follow you on social media and start engaging with your content, subscribe to your mailing list, browse your products or services online or attend one of your events. They've taken the next step in getting to know you better. It's at this point you should be looking to foster your relationship further. This is where your Clapping Collins and Megaphone Mandys are hanging out.

- Bottom of funnel: this is where you want to get them to – they buy from you, subscribe to your membership or book onto your course and eventually they repeat-buy, talk about you at their book clubs and introduce their friends to you. A big mistake I see businesses make is getting their audiences through to the last stage and then doing absolutely nothing to keep them engaged. We're going to talk about retention later on in Chapter 9. Your Diehard Dennises and OG Olgas are here with you.

All of this requires work and effort and needs time to grow and evolve organically.

Let's break the levels down further into the five phases you need to look at holistically when working on your own strategy:

THE REALITIES OF BUILDING AN ONLINE COMMUNITY

AWARENESS: PEACOCKING

Dating: this is where you hit the club, join a dating app or a new sports team to get as many eyes on you or your profile as possible when recruiting a new love interest.

Business: the same principle applies – top of funnel is all about reaching new audiences and getting new eyes or visitors on your business. It's the first stage in your audience's journey before they go on to become advocates and part of your community and where you start to work your charm on your Lingering Lindas.

INTEREST: THE FLIRTING STAGE

Dating: you've hit the club, football team or dating app of your choice and found someone you're digging. They like the same snacks as you, have a great playlist they've shared with you and support the same political party. Right now their Dad jokes are quite funny and you've started to turn up the heat with some very clichéd chat-up lines.

Business: your new potential community member has landed on your social media channels, blog or website and they're into what you're about. Your branding speaks to them and what you said in your brand bio resonated with them. At this point, Clapping Collin is giving you the eye and, dare I say it, you're flirting.

DESIRE: WINING & DINING
Dating: dad-joke love-interest person has invited you out on a date. They've pulled out all of the stops too: dinner, drinks *and* a movie. Someone get this person a medal immediately.

Business: you're nurturing your audience with desirable content. At this point, it's about selling in your business values and unique story to get them on board and keep up the momentum. Megaphone Mandy has a full-blown crush at this point; she's even told her mates about you.

ACTION: MAKING IT OFFICIAL
Dating: it's official. You've featured them on your social media profiles and the heart-eye emojis are coming in thick and fast on the new picture you posted of you two together at your old school friend's wedding.

Business: you got a sale/sign-up/booking. They're officially on board and on the way to becoming a Diehard Dennis.

COMMUNITY: TYING THE KNOT
Dating: you're theirs for life. You wear matching Christmas jumpers, finish each other's sentences and know exactly how to wind them up, but goodness me, you can't imagine life without them. You sing their praises all the time, take them everywhere you go and tell your friends all about them.

Business: they're committed; they will never buy from a competitor again. They sign up to your newsletters to hear about your latest news and are the first to support you when it's announced. They share your content and tell their friends about you. They follow you around the city when you're hosting events or doing pop-ups. They engage with your content, join your communities outside of social media and talk to other fans of the brand. Your OG Olgas have joined the groupie gang and they're officially in love.

There is a deeper-rooted communication strategy and a whole ride your audience needs to go on before you attempt to convert them into long-standing community advocates. When planning your content, along with pillars and purpose, it's important to be aware of what stage of the journey you want to be promoting and focusing on. You can absolutely be recruiting new community members at different stages, you just need to make sure that this journey is seamless.

Remember my behind-the-scenes example from the last chapter (see page 120)? The storytelling content didn't convert straight away, but over time, with increased brand awareness, it sure did. When looking at your funnel, remember that it's a journey – you can't Amazon Prime your way to growth; it's not an overnight process.

It's important to refer back to your channels of choice and think about where they sit within the hierarchy. For example, you may start a podcast that is also repurposed into a YouTube channel to help with your discovery. Once you've nailed YouTube and your podcast and feel comfortable with expanding your reach, you could then use LinkedIn, TikTok and Instagram to share more of the day-to-day life of your business and drive people to your website and newsletter to share more about your products or services. You'll also need to remember how your audience changes on the different platforms, as we discussed in Chapter 3, and what kind of content you're going to create to engage them and migrate them down the funnel. I have found that physically drawing a diagram like the one I've used on page 148 can be super helpful. I've also provided a template tool that you can use to create your funnel in the resources hub.

EXAMPLES OF GOOD BRAND-TO-COMMUNITY FLIRTING

GETTING SINGLES TOGETHER WITHOUT THE 'CRINGE'

If, like me, the idea of online dating makes you want to retreat into a burrow far underground with nothing but a torch and a lifetime's supply of popcorn and doughnuts, then it sounds like you're not alone because it turns out there's a dating app that gets our struggle too.

Thursday is an app designed for singles who want to take the awkwardness out of online dating. The concept is simple: the app only works on a Thursday and it often hosts IRL events for its community to attend so that they can meet new (and single) people in one place. Its tag line is 'we met on Thursday', a way to combat the stigma and awkwardness around meeting people online.

Thursday often uses out-of-home PR stunts to raise brand awareness: examples include interns chaining themselves to street lamps while holding DIY cardboard signs saying, 'World's most embarrassing internship. Single? Download *Thursday*. #Cuffing Season.' It has a huge presence across multiple social media platforms and its employees are ambassadors for the brand. They often go viral on LinkedIn for their shares on company culture and behind-the-scenes content. *Thursday* has built a strong reputation in both the business-to-business and business-to-consumer spaces through its tongue-in-cheek messaging. It often calls out competitors and creates controversial marketing which has massively increased its brand awareness.

Thursday creates content that addresses its community's pain points by highlighting the awkward side of online dating and meeting via apps, and offers them a solution. The content is highly relatable and touches upon Gen Z and millennial cultural moments which creates a link between the brand and its audience. The fact that the app is only available to use one day of the week creates scarcity and enhances desire. The product is also completely tailored to the brand's community's needs and requirements.

As a business, *Thursday* is growing its own first-party data (first-party data = data that **you** own) efforts without relying on social media apps to cultivate its community. Having app downloads and active users in its community means that it isn't reliant on algorithms and third-party sources to reach the right people. It has the app to communicate with its audience and incentivises downloads by offering them the chance to connect with like-minded individuals who have the same purpose: finding a match.

Thursday accelerates the growth of its community by offering meet-up events for singles and opportunities to make URL inter-actions into IRL ones in a space with the wider community.

LESSONS WE CAN LEARN FROM *THURSDAY* WHEN IT COMES TO BUILDING FUNNELS

- Creating disruptive content that is organically shared will aid in word-of-mouth referrals and grow awareness.
- Encouraging your employees to participate in your content will help humanise your online presence and build a rapport with your community.
- Hopping on culturally relevant moments that pique the interest of your community and audience will help show them you've got your finger on the pulse.
- Clearly demonstrating the solution to an audience's problem will incentivise the end goal.
- Creating an offline environment for your community to come together and connect will augment your efforts in forming a strong sense of connectivity.
- Monitoring your community's values and ensuring yours align will spark a connection.
- Building intimate spaces will help you foster an engaged community who have aligned values.
- Don't plug all of your efforts in to social media. Be sure to look at growing your first-party data too.

CREATING AN OPEN AND VULNERABLE SPACE
FOR FEMALE FOUNDERS TO CONNECT

Babes on Waves is a membership and community for female founders in the creative industry, specifically people of colour. The membership offers talks, workshops and events for members to attend and learn about the lessons of running a side hustle or business. Workshops span from finance through to brand partnerships.

Babes on Waves utilises brand partnerships to increase awareness and has collaborated with brands such as Reebok, ASOS and Converse. It also works with its community, many of whom are micro influencers on collaborative social media content to help spread the word on the work that it does.

Within its social media content Babes on Waves addresses the challenges that come with being a female founder and speaks directly to its ideal community's pain points. Its branding is brightly coloured and visually appealing, aligning with its creative audience's wants and needs. It incentivises potential community members with exclusive workshops, events and access to other creatives sharing advice and collaboration opportunities.

Outside of social media, members are invited to a Slack channel, moderated by community managers who are there specifically to encourage conversation and talking points. There are different channels and threads that the community can engage with, such as 'opportunities', 'wins' and 'IRL meet-ups'.

LESSONS WE CAN LEARN FROM BABES ON WAVES
WHEN IT COMES TO BUILDING FUNNELS

- Pull on your existing community to create content and spread your awareness.
- Look to source aligned partnerships to increase your visibility within new spaces (there's a whole chapter on collaborations coming up).
- Ensure that your branding stands out and magnetises the right audiences.

- Offer exclusive and gated content as a way to increase hype and additional motivations for sign-ups. Gated content = content that typically requires users to share their information (usually name and email address) to access exclusive content such as reports, videos and content that isn't available to the wider public. It is usually sent to the user once they've filled in a form.
- Create a space where you can facilitate conversations for your community to speak to each other and form genuine connections outside of traditional apps.

Both examples are the perfect demonstration of using the community journey, taking them from awareness (aka peacocking) through to tying the knot (aka community). Using a variety of content spanning partnerships and collaborations through to content that resonates and intimate spaces such as events, apps and Slack channels, both businesses have successfully built blossoming communities.

TAKING THE DREAM FAR AND WIDE

If you're looking to spread your message far and wide, beyond traditional social media apps, it's so important that you treat your channels holistically. Paid ads should work in alignment with your social media channels; your messaging and promotions should be consistent.

Equally, when pitching yourself for PR and podcasts it's important that the topics you pitch are relevant to your overall brand message and purpose.

PODCASTS
Podcasts tend to be evergreen, which means the content stays relevant and valuable for a long period of time. The great thing about podcasts is that they tend to be more story- and

conversation-focused. They're also a great way for your community to hear you speak about your passions and add a human touch to your work. A few years ago I pitched myself to speak on a podcast in the US with one of my favourite creators, Katie Steckly, and it increased my following and presence across the pond, and I even secured a one-to-one strategy client off the back of it.

FIVE TIPS FOR PITCHING YOURSELF TO PODCASTS

1. Research the host and look at previous guests to look for any specific themes or topics that you can add value to or avoid crossing over.
2. Offer three ideas that you can speak confidently about.
3. Ask them if they'd like to have a phone call to discuss the ideas.
4. Give them times and dates when you're able to record.
5. Try to find an email address rather than direct messaging them. Often social media messages can get lost.

PRESS COVERAGE

Press coverage can be invaluable for growing your brand awareness and reaching new audiences. Having press features is also great for building up your credibility as a business, and the good news is you don't need a little black book of journalists – it's no longer a 'who-you-know' industry. With the rise in digital media and publications, journalists are constantly seeking quotes and stories from people just like you.

FIVE TIPS FOR PITCHING YOURSELF TO PRESS

1. Look at the topics the publication or media features and find a journalist who is reporting on stories within your niche. (LinkedIn is a great place to find journalists.)
2. Keep messages succinct and to the point. Journalists are super busy: introduce yourself, summarise your story and why you think it would be of interest and provide your contact details.

3. You can check Twitter for the # journorequests where journalists often ask for quotes and stories.
4. Keep an eye on what is trending in the press and think about how you can contribute to this. (This is called newsjacking and it's a very effective way to grow your awareness.)

5. Attach a press release to your email, if you have one, to give the journalist more insight into your pitch should they find it of interest.

As with all marketing channels, you shouldn't rely solely on one platform to drive your revenue and grow your business. You need to think about where all of the channels fit within your overall strategy and how you're going to get your Lingering Lindas down to your Diehard Dennises.

CREATING EMOTIVE CONTENT THAT CONNECTS

After I'd graduated from university, my first role out in the big ol' grown-up world was in a creative agency where I was managing multiple client accounts at one time and learning how to 'schmooze'. As the new digital account executive, it was my job to organise the Christmas party for one of our biggest accounts. At this point, I didn't live in London and so didn't know where the hotspots were. After a bit of googling, I found a few places and booked dinner and drinks. Much to my dismay, the place I'd booked for drinks turned out to be an old pub on the corner of an alleyway. The floor was sticky, the glasses were dusty and the staff could not have made it more obvious that they were hungover and did not want to be there. As if it couldn't get any worse, as the clients turned up, a heavy rock band began rehearsing in the dingy basement where we were sitting. I was horrified. One of our biggest clients was sitting opposite me – they were renowned for being difficult to please and I was so eager to impress them. I could tell from their raised eyebrows that they were, in fact, not impressed. We had to shout over each other because the bass was so loud and, by this point, I was a deep shade of purple. It gets worse.

After leaving the intimate rock concert, we made our way to dinner. Fortunately, the restaurant was great and the food and cocktails were amazing. Things were going really well until I headed to the bathroom and bumped into the waiter behind me . . . and, subsequently, they dropped a plate of food all over the client's *very* expensive jacket. I won't divulge the details of what happened next because it genuinely makes me shudder, but I made a very quick exit after that.

Still purple with embarrassment, I stood on the station platform waiting for my train to get me the hell out of London. It was pouring with rain so I was soaked and looking extremely sorry for myself, like something from a low-budget romcom. I looked up and saw an advert for Sweaty Betty. There was no imagery and no sign of any product, just a few sentences that read 'take out your phone, think of someone you love and send them three reasons why you love them'. Their logo was on the advert along with a #. I took a picture of the billboard and texted my best friend with the three reasons why I loved her.

The campaign was genius. Not only was Sweaty Betty encouraging conversation with its community and raising awareness of its brand, it was building an emotional connection with its audience, and research concludes that emotion is the biggest driver of loyalty in many industries.[1]

Some businesses translate this approach in the online space by creating shareable content that proactively encourages people to share and discuss with their community. A self-help coach may upload a video offering confidence advice and caption it 'tag someone who needs to see this'; a travel brand may upload an aspirational travel picture with the caption 'who would you share this moment with?'; a restaurant may share its new cocktail list with 'drop your funniest margarita memory below and we'll pick a winner': the point is you're encouraging conversation and, don't forget, people want to feel part of your world.

How can you weave in calls to action that are more about connection and not just sales? If you're already using social media, you'll know that, quite often, the comments section is more of a party than the content itself – people will leave comments such as 'anyone else RUN to the comments?' or 'fell over sprinting to the comments' because the conversations and exchanges can often be more entertaining and funnier than the videos themselves, with users exchanging sentiments, thoughts and jokes.

It's not just product-based businesses that can encourage this kind of participation and emotive content. I've seen LinkedInfluencers (yes, that's a thing) write statuses asking their community to leave a comment about a time when someone inspired them, recommended them for a job or helped them with their career and tag the person who inspired them. Again, they're tapping into the sentiment and emotions of their audience. Most importantly, they're talking to one another and the LinkedInfluencer is facilitating conversation which therefore creates a psychological bond and connection with said LinkedInfluencer through creating a positive conversation via their platform.

This concept can manifest in many ways. Many fitness gurus create Facebook groups for their communities to encourage each other and stay accountable; wellness businesses host retreats; and gaming companies gather communities via Twitch. And there's a good reason for this – 78 per cent of consumers want brands to use social media to help people connect with each other.[2] Who can blame us? We're only human, after all. As we spoke about in Chapter 6 when we discussed intimate spaces, **it's important that you reflect what makes sense for your community when thinking about how to facilitate these connections**.

HARNESSING THE POWER OF TESTIMONIALS AND REVIEWS

In the early stages of your business, your reviews and testimonials are going to be paramount for building trust and belief in what you do. Sadly, you can't just walk around with an internet megaphone shouting about how great you are and expect people to buy it anymore. As we've already seen, your community will be snooping on the conversations people are having about you before they even think about committing to the sign-up or sale.

With this in mind, it's so important that you start collecting testimonials and reviews, and sharing examples of when you took your customers 'from X to Y'. Whenever I finish a project with a client I ask for a testimonial as part of my off-boarding process. It's at this point that I ask the following questions:

- How did you feel before working with me?
- How did you feel about the process?
- What results did you see after?
- How did you feel after?

I can harness the power of storytelling here and tell my community where my clients started and where I got them to. I can share tangible results, which is far more effective than me shouting about how brilliant I am all of the time. Software such as Trustpilot and Google My Business can also help with your organic search ranking.

Tip: make collecting testimonials and reviews part of your sales process. You could prompt them with an email after buying a product or ask for a LinkedIn recommendation. Make it as easy as possible for them to leave you a review as people are often busy and forget.

After my first year in business, I knew I wanted to move away from full social media management and transition into a strategy offer. I knew that I was going to need testimonials to advertise my new services, so I offered an introduction offer to some of my OG Olgas and previous clients and used it as a testing ground for my new service. It was an opportunity to gather feedback so that I could enhance the service for my community and collect testimonials to help me drive interest.

So, why are testimonials so effective?

- They're unbiased.
- They're less 'icky' and 'salesy' than a marketing pitch.
- People trust other consumers more than they trust businesses.
- They increase your credibility.

Start thinking about how you can collect your own testimonials. Could you use a third-party site like Trustpilot? Can you set up some automated emails? Can you design an off-boarding process for clients and include this as part of the procedure?

Collecting testimonials and reviews isn't just about having evidence that your business is transformational; they can also be used as content. Some businesses will use funny tweets and brand mentions and repurpose them into content or share user-generated content to their feeds (don't worry – we're going to talk about this in the next chapter).

Now you should have a clear understanding of your community journey, you should be thinking about how to design your own funnel and the ways in which you'll migrate your Lindas into Dennises and retain your Olgas into long-lasting advocates. Next up we're going to talk about one of my favourite parts of community-building: collaboration, and the different ways that you can start to think about how you can run successful collaborations for your own business.

CHAPTER RECAP

- Fostering an engaged community needs work, the same way dating and friendship do. Remember to keep in mind that your community will all be at different stages. Don't just focus on growth – keep in mind how you're going to retain your Olgas.
- Build out your channels into an ecosystem and plan how you will migrate your community through the funnel.
- Create an outreach list of different podcasts and media you could pitch yourself to. Think about the main story you want to be known for and how you could start to tell it.
- Think about how you can start to embed reviews and testimonials into your process.

Chapter 8

DON'T HATE, COLLABORATE

'Audiences are siloed into tiny niches,
and everyone's algorithm is so
different so, without collaborations,
or at least meaningful ways for
audiences to share what a business
or creative does, it is very difficult to
build any traction. Collaboration is
a way of having a conversation and
ideas not being fixed.'

Elijah, founder of Close the
App, Make the Thing

In this chapter, we'll look at the importance of collaboration to help position your offer, raise your awareness and tap into new communities to help grow your existing one. We will discuss business-to-business collaborations, as well as collaborating with your community to fuel business decisions and generate content.

COLLABORATION IS KING

Back in the day when interacting with brands and businesses, consumers would form bonds through sexy advertising and engaging with their products. However, social media has opened many doors for businesses and we now have the opportunity to not only talk to our communities, we can also collaborate with them.

As well as collaborating with our Diehard Dennises and Lingering Lindas, we can also collaborate with creators and other businesses that align with our values. The social media platforms have given us all a space to interact with our fans and followers in ways we could have never imagined before. New features are constantly being rolled out in a bid to blossom relationships among fans and followers alike.

The word collaboration used to be associated with rappers joining forces or big brands like Coca-Cola sponsoring football teams and award shows. Nowadays, collaborations go so much further than that: collaborations take place between brands and their customers; photographers form partnerships with brand experts to create packages for their clients; and brands once perceived as competitors come together to create products for their communities. Utilising the power of collaboration shows your community that you're socially active, you're hanging out in other internet neighbourhoods and you're welcoming other communities into your neighbourhood too. As we know already, brands are like people and what do people want? Connection.

So what could a collaboration look like for you? It could be that you partner with your community to create content using your products or service. It could be that you work with another brand to create a limited-edition product or a signature offer. It could be that you work with a creator or influencer who aligns with your brand to amplify your message. There are multiple ways that you can weave collaboration into your community building strategy. Collaborations can come in many different shapes and sizes; however, the benefits are plentiful:

- Reach and awareness: you get the opportunity to share your magic with new audiences who align with your values and could go on to become loyal advocates once you've taken them through your community journey (see Chapter 7).
- Endorse community involvement: collaborating with your community gives you the opportunity to amplify their voices through your own content. No one wants to participate in digital interactions that aren't a two-way street these days. There are

endless ways for you to implement community involvement into your strategy, which we will talk about later in this chapter.

- Create cultural relevance: collaborating with other brands, creators or community members allows you to reposition yourself among the communities that you want your business to be seen within.
- Active conversation-starters: partnerships often spread through word-of-mouth advocacy and encourage your community to share with their own communities too.
- Grow your credibility: partnering with your community will show your other community members that you're committed to involving them in your journey and process, which will make them feel validated and cared for by you.
- They're good old-fashioned fun: lock me up and call me basic, but collaborations are also super fun. They allow you to get creative and work alongside others to create new content, work in new ways and meet new people.

COLLABORATION CRITERIA

Before you head off and dive into collaboration mode, there are some criteria you should be aware of first:

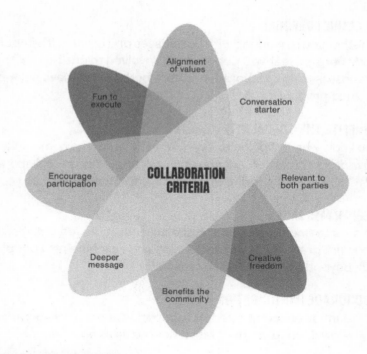

The diagram shows "COLLABORATION CRITERIA" at the center with petals labeled: Alignment of values, Conversation starter, Relevant to both parties, Creative freedom, Benefits the community, Deeper message, Encourage participation, Fun to execute.

ALIGNMENT OF VALUES

Whether you're collaborating with another business, creator or someone in your community, there needs to be an alignment of values. For example, a fast-fashion brand collaborating with a sustainable style influencer wouldn't land because their values are out of sync and both the brand's and influencer's communities will see through it.

CONVERSATION STARTER

Crocs were able to reposition themselves from style disaster to footwear must-have because their collaborations were strategic and got people talking. They've collaborated with other cool fashion brands, rappers and even KFC! All of their collaborations were interesting and encouraged hype.

RELEVANT TO BOTH PARTIES

Ensuring there is equal benefit to both collaborators is key. Make sure you're aware of what your collaborator will gain from partnering with you. This is especially important when you're pitching and proposing the collaboration to them: what do they get from this?

CREATIVE FREEDOM

Whether you're working with businesses or a creator, it's important there is creative freedom for all involved to ensure that the
process is truly collaborative. Ensure both parties have a say in
the end product.

BENEFITS THE COMMUNITY

You know what I'm going to say . . . What's in it for the community?
How do both parties' communities benefit from the collaboration? What does this bring to their lives and interactions with you?

DEEPER MESSAGE

Be sure to find the purpose in the collaboration. Yes, collaborations are great for brand awareness and reaching new people,
but, beyond that, what is the reason for this?

ENCOURAGE PARTICIPATION

How can you encourage people to participate in the collaboration
and allow them to connect with it beyond sales and revenue?

FUN TO EXECUTE

Above all else, collaborating should be fun! It's an opportunity
for you to connect with other businesses and people, try something completely new and get creative.

USING COLLABORATION AS A FORCE FOR GOOD

In 2020, the global Covid-19 pandemic hit and many of us were
unable to draw the line between work and home, spending
hours glued to our devices, while others were trying to fill the
days with Pinterest-inspired cheese-fondue recipes, endless
WhatsApp groups and scrolling through social media feeds to
remain connected with the world.

I remember observing this from my own screen: I tuned into the
sentiment of my own community – blurry eyes filled Instagram
lives, a heavy tone swept across the comments sections of YouTube

vlogs and TikTok's viral dance challenges had transitioned into mental-health hubs and tired commentary about the pandemic. Many were talking about the intense digital fatigue they were feeling – a sense of numbness, disassociation and lack of hope. It seemed that the reality of working from home and blurring the lines between home and work had caught up with everyone.

I started to think about my own mental health as well as that of those around me, and decided to take a day off, away from my screen, my phone and the TV. By this point, we were allowed outside, so I took my backpack, filled it with books, notepads, snacks and a jumper, and left my tiny London flat and headed to the greenery and trees by the river. I remember tears rolling down my face as I walked out of the door, not because I was sad but because I felt free. Free from the shackles of my devices that, in all honesty, felt more like a second pair of hands at that point – finally I was away from the notifications. As I took my backpack off my shoulder and sat on the grass, I remember feeling a huge sense of relief. That's where the phrase 'check yourself before your notifications' was birthed.

The next day, I ran polls on my Instagram story to gauge how people were feeling. I opened up space in my private Facebook group, spoke to my community through voice notes and sent an email relaying my own personal experience, to which I received an overwhelming response saying people felt the same.

The following week, I sent a proposal to the mental-health charity Mind and asked them if they'd like to partner on a collaboration to raise money for those struggling with their mental health. We got on a call, I told them about the conversations I'd been having and they told me about the shocking increase they'd seen in mental-health cases since the start of the pandemic. We agreed a partnership there and then.

I created jumpers, prints and phone cases in my branding with the words 'check yourself before your notifications' on them. I took pictures of the products at home in my very dimly lit flat and created a landing page and products on my website using

Squarespace Commerce (Squarespace is a website building company with an eCommerce feature which allows you to sell products). Within three weeks of my initial conversation with Mind, I had a website ready to go. This was the most significant project I'd worked on – it was so personal and it felt important to me so I really wanted to make the campaign as impactful as possible.

The merch sold out within one week and I had to reorder more, meaning more money for the charity and an amazing launch that got people talking about a topic that was very close to my heart and my own brand values. It felt so rewarding to know that people were opening up the conversation.

So, why was the collaboration so successful within my community?

SHARING IS CARING

While in pre-launch mode, I built up lots of hype and awareness on my channels by sharing behind-the-scenes content with my community. I took them on the journey of my design process and asked them to vote for their favourite designs. I then used their responses and the data from them to put the most popular designs into production. As a one-man-band, my budgets weren't huge and I bootstrapped the entire campaign, which meant that the products were limited. I also needed to sell the first batch of product to pay for the next round, so I created a pre-sale sign-up form on my website for my community to opt in to a newsletter list where they would go on to be the first to hear about the campaign and the first to shop the limited-edition stock.

COMMUNITY INVOLVEMENT

I wanted to bring my community into the campaign and create content that was both valuable and supportive. I knew my newsletter community were super engaged with my intimate projects – I often used it as a space to share more personal sentiments and updates and had always received a great response. I asked my newsletter community to share with me the ways that they switched off from social media and brought peace and balance to their lives, and hundreds of responses flew in, ranging from meditation apps, tapping therapies, hot chocolate recipes, books, poets, self-care rituals and exercise regimes. I selected a diverse range of responses and applied them to an Instagram filter I had created to promote the campaign.

SHAREABILITY

The person using the filter would be presented with animated text which said 'check yourself before your notifications' which would appear on their heads when opening the filter. When they tapped the screen the responses would flick up and alternate quickly before landing on a random phrase submitted by my community. I shared the filter which had both my own logo and Mind's with my community and asked them to share it far and wide. The filter went down extremely well and had a reach of over 10,000 uses, which was much bigger than the number of followers I had at the time. Due to the interactive nature of the filter, plus the fact that there was an educational and valuable takeaway to go with it, it spread very quickly.

CONNECTEDNESS

Throughout the campaign launch, I shared imagery and videos of the product and also peppered in educational and valuable content on the topic of digital well-being with my community. I shared the responses I had used in the filter as carousel posts and tagged the people who had shared their thoughts so that their submissions were validated and recognised. Most of the people who had contributed shared the campaign with their own networks and communities which aided awareness of the campaign, meaning my OG Olgas were reaching my Lingering Lindas through advocacy, raising more awareness for Mind.

I let my community participate in something they felt deeply connected to. Remember when we spoke about values and the importance of aligning yours with theirs in Chapter 2 (see page 34)? This is a prime example of utilising aligned values and allowing your community to participate in your projects and work. I attribute the success of that campaign to my community. If I hadn't worked on building my community and passing the mic to them, I probably wouldn't have sold half as much of the merch and it would have been a flop.

How could you utilise the power of collaboration to drive change and bring your community together? Refer back to your sweet spot exercise and your community-values work we discussed in Chapter 2. Write down all of the different causes you could support and the businesses that align with yours and could back you in bringing your communities together for good.

Most importantly, your collaborations should be deeply aligned to your higher mission and purpose. Always make sure you conduct thorough research into the person/brands/creators you decide to partner with to ensure your synergy runs deep.

USER-GENERATED CONTENT

We used to trust our friends and family to make recommendations: recipes, films, holiday destinations, clothes, microwaves and everything else in between. In more recent times, we've resorted to the internet to research brands and their credibility. In fact, according to one study, 90 per cent of consumers say that user-generated content (UGC) influences their buying decisions more than any other form of advertising.[1] Who can blame us? It's content that we haven't had to pay for and has been willingly posted by our community because they're satisfied with their experience of a brand.

Something that I always look for now when researching a business is tagged content submitted by existing customers. I want to understand the legitimacy: are people buying this product? Are they enjoying it? More importantly, are they advocating for it? Because if they're doing the latter, you know the business has worked to get some Diehard Dennises on its side, and if it's got Diehard Dennises, you know it's doing something very right.

Maximising UGC has become a popular technique among those fostering communities online. Before we dive into why you should harness the power of UGC, let's outline the different types:

CUSTOMERS/CLIENTS

A lot of UGC will come naturally through your customers or clients advocating for what you do. This is one of the most authentic, low-cost and effective ways to create content and it also helps to form a deeper connection with the rest of your audience. They will naturally tag you and mention you in videos or images if they like your product or service.

Coffee brand Starbucks receives hundreds of tagged pieces of content per day. It's positioned its brand as an accessory and has even created merchandise with distinguishable branding across it so that its products and drinks are immediately recognised in its feeds (Refer back to Chapter 1 to refresh your memory on visual identity). Starbucks merchandise often appears in TikTok videos, and many creators film content from the Starbucks drive-throughs.

It also helps that Starbucks has been coined as the glamorous option for coffee and is often spotted in films and influencer paparazzi pictures. Its community wants to be a part of the aspirational image it has obtained and organically advocate for the brand, which, in turn, makes it feel more trusted and the community feels part of something.

WAYS TO ENCOURAGE THIS
- Use a branded # across your own social media channels. You could also look to have this included on any printed communications and in any physical spaces where you operate.
- Reshare your community content in a round-up or on your feeds so that your community feels valued, sees other advocates and, in tandem, chooses to share more.
- Feature existing customers on your website and other communications. Remember that, as well as helping you build trust with your community, testimonials and reviews can also count as a form of UGC (see page 172). If you're a service provider, remember to ensure that testimonials are part of your client process.

> - Ask your clients/customers. When I run events, I create shareable moments and, on my slides, I always remind my community to share their experience online and tag me if they enjoyed it so that I can connect with them via social media afterwards.

UGC CREATORS

Many brands now employ creators on a freelance basis to create content for them month on month. They're not social media managers or influencers; they're creators who are paid to create a consistent stream of content for the brand to build familiarity and humanise their feeds.

Later Media is a technology company that allows people running social media accounts to schedule their social media posts and create analytics reports within their software. Later Media has vibrant branding that stands out on feeds and a personable approach to its content. It works with UGC creators on a retained basis to create video content. Seeing the same faces in its content helps build familiarity and a human feel which builds a rapport with its community. Later Media often shares content about the struggles of being a social media manager and the constant battle of algorithm updates which enhances its relatability with its community and builds a deeper connection. Later Media's content often sparks conversation among its community in the comments section. By sharing its own personal stories and experiences that its community can also relate to, it kick-starts a conversation which encourages its followers and community to bond.

WAYS TO IMPLEMENT THIS
- Use #s and search terms related to your product to get a feel for the type of content people are creating in your space.

- Look for creators who are creating their own organic content and align with your brand and reach out to them about content-creation opportunities. It's worth noting that creators with a higher following will typically be more expensive. However, there is now a trend in micro influencer collaborations and the great news is, they're often far more cost-effective and won't mean big bucks.

INFLUENCERS AND CREATORS

Influencer marketing and creator partnerships is not a new concept and the industry continues to grow year on year with more brands plugging spend into influencer partnerships than ever before. Why? Because they know that their communities are more likely to trust real people versus adverts. However, we are seeing a rise in brands tapping into 'creators' (not UGC creators, just creators), who typically harness the power of subcultures (see page 51) due to the more niche nature of their content. The two are often confused, so refer back to page 122 to understand the difference.

Brands know that consumers want more than pretty pictures and someone they can relate to. As we wise up to marketing and consumerism, we want the partnerships we see online to reflect the visions of both parties. These kind of influencers have been coined by *Vogue* as 'genuinfluencers': they have more longevity and effectiveness because the partnerships we're seeing feel more real.[2]

Adobe is a software company that creates applications spanning video editing and illustration tools through to 3D animation and often shares tutorials for its audience to help them improve the use of its software. Adobe works with creators and educators in the creative industry to create valuable and educational content for its own communities and for it to share on its pages. The partnerships feel authentic as the influencers Adobe works with are already sharing valuable content, so it feels less like a sales tactic for both parties and the influencers will already have buy-in and support from their communities because the content feels like an authentic fit.

WAYS TO IMPLEMENT THIS
- Search for tagged content in your niche. Look out for partnerships within your industry to get a feel for the creators who are already out there.
- Use #s to search for keywords within your niche and make use of social media SEO to discover content relating to your industry.
- Look for talent agencies that work with creators who represent talent with meaningful purpose.

When considering the above, it's important to ensure the people you are partnering with align with your selfhood, your bigger picture and also your community values. How do they fit into your sweet spot (see page 56)? Can you see them in there? Would it feel authentic for your community to see them there? Often, brands jump to partnerships because the collaborator has lots of followers, when really a better metric to look at is the engagement rate. This is the true indicator of how engaged someone's community really is. You can find out how to work out the engagement rate in the resources hub.

Finally, when using other people's content it's always polite to ask if they're happy for you to reshare. If you're paying them for the content, ensure that you're clear within your agreement and outline where the content will be used, (for example, if you want to use the content in your paid advertising campaigns) and always credit the creator and original source.

INVOLVING THE COMMUNITY

Beyond relying on UGC and depending on your customers to submit their content, there are ways you can proactively start to collaborate with your community to get them involved with your content and campaigns. This is by far one of the most original and legitimate ways to build an affinity between you and your community.

PROACTIVE ENGAGEMENT
Keeping in touch with your community is absolutely crucial for understanding their sentiments and knowing how they're feeling. This should go way beyond reading comments and messages – you should be proactively starting conversations and involving them in your products and offers.

Many of the social media platforms now house features such as polls and quizzes where you can ask your community for feedback and get them to vote on products. This not only works wonders for your engagement as your community will be proactively participating in your content, but it will also give you the gold dust of insight into how you can level up and serve your community through direct conversations. Of course, it is important that you utilise the platforms we discussed in Chapter 5 (see page 79) and do external research too. However, having genuine conversations and truly talking to your community OGs will have a huge impact in the development of your offer, and it will also strengthen your bond with them.

Elsie & Fred is a women's e-commerce brand targeting Gen Z and millennial women and non-binary people. Its mission is to help them celebrate their own individuality through the medium of expression in clothing. The three founders are very present and active within the business and in their social media campaigns, often at the forefront of brand-focused content and holding interactive conversations with their community.

They often share sketches and illustrations before products reach production and share behind-the-scenes snippets of upcoming collections and ask their community to vote on colourways, prints and designs. They use that feedback to design their collections. This works incredibly well as they have foresight of the appetite from their community, and their community feels satisfied knowing that their opinions are heard and proactively implemented.

Estrid is a razor brand championing all body types. It has an exceptionally engaged community and often gets them involved with naming the products, and rewarding them with products in exchange, giving them an incentive to engage with one another.

Vix Meldrew is an educator who supports service providers in becoming better educators and guides them with course builds and education programmes. When teasing out her own courses and new offers, she gauges the appetite from her community by sharing initial thoughts and brain dumps of her new offers to determine the demand for what she's ideating before going to the length of investing and planning. By predetermining the appetite from her community through conversations, polls and quizzes, she's able to establish whether her new offer is worth pursuing or not.

Start thinking about how you can encourage participation from your community. Can you make use of interactive features such as polls and quizzes or ask them for their opinions on your upcoming programmes or products and use this insight to deliver what they truly want? How can you include your community in your process and make them feel valued? Make a list of all of the participation techniques you could use for your upcoming launches and general content concepts.

Tip: when looking to source UGC from your community specifically, there's no better way than to simply ask. If they're advocates, they'll be more willing to share content with their own communities too.

CROWDSOURCING
As we've already seen, as humans we connect to storytelling. We're nosy, we like to know what's up, we're intrigued. It's why people flock to the tabloids, head to Twitter to find

out the latest goss and observe how others are reacting to information.

In recent years, brands have harnessed the power of real stories and have begun crowdsourcing their content. Crowdsourcing is when brands and creators ask their communities to share their own stories and turn the real-story submissions into content. This works for many different reasons:

1. You get to champion your fans.
2. It saves you time ideating.
3. Your community gets to connect with others in your community and relate to their stories.
4. It's an authentic way to show your community that you're talking to them.
5. It's highly relatable because it's come from a real person.

Bumble is a dating app that shares real stories from its community. It will ask them about their worst first-date stories, their dating red flags (and green ones) and their favourite first-date ideas. It takes this information and turns it into content, whether it's video story-time content from creators or documentary-style series capturing real couples sharing their own stories. This resonates with other users of the app who have similar stories, helping them to realise they're not alone in their experiences too.

A financial well-being app that supports women with investing and financial education, bridging the gap in the finance space between men and women, *Your Juno* asks its community to anonymously submit their job titles, salary and a breakdown of their monthly outgoings. It shares this with its community. This content gives its existing community a window into a typically very taboo subject, and sparks engagement and often controversy, which gets its community talking. It also helps the existing community get a feel for a subject that is typically shied away from and can feel confrontational.

Think about how you can start to utilise real stories, thoughts and opinions to amplify your community's voices. Let's say you're a confidence coach: you could look to ask your community what and who makes them feel most confident and share ways in which they could implement the crowdsourced advice. It could be that you make cookies for special occasions: you could ask your community what their favourite nostalgic pudding is and create a retro spin-off series. The sky really is the limit, but the beauty of this exercise is that it allows you to magnify the thoughts from your community while fuelling your own content with unique stories and perspectives.

HARNESS DATA

Another great way that brands source information is by looking at the data from their communities and their behavioural habits. *Spotify* is a music-streaming app that allows you to listen to your favourite music and podcasts. At the end of each year, it releases Spotify Wrapped, a personalised feature that shows its users what songs they listened to most, their favourite artists, genres and also summarises the whole thing with a music personality type. The wrap up is highly shareable and year on year it prompts a ripple effect across social media, with users sharing their own *Spotify* Wrapped with friends and followers. It's gone on to create funny tongue-in-cheek out-of-home campaigns using the data, creating billboards that say things such as, 'Dear person who played "Sorry" 42 times on Valentine's Day – what did you do?' Admittedly, *Spotify* has a wealth of data to play with and can dig deep to create these funny and captivating campaigns, but applying this principal is a very effective way for you to share the thoughts of your own community too.

DUST OFF YOUR POM-POMS

Everyone loves a cheerleader. As humans, we all need them. Recognition is a big part of our lives. When I was at school I was terrible at maths, terrible. But I had a teacher who really believed in me and helped me improve and, from then on, I felt committed to doing her proud and worked extra hard in her classes. The positive reinforcement from her made me want to do better and she will always be one of my favourite teachers.

The same principle goes for your community: if you commit to cheerleading for them and celebrating them, they will feel more inclined to support your quest and cheerlead for you in return. Spotlighting their success is a huge win for them. We've seen this with dairy substitute milk brand Oatly, which made a documentary about a man in the States who created a boat using Oatly bottles. Anti-diet fitness app *Nobs* uses members of its community to be the face of the brand in photoshoots and shares their stories through social media. Fashion brand Lazy Oaf gives its community the opportunity to showcase their creative talents through an interview series on their 'Oaf World' blog.

Tip: by passing the mic to your community and illuminating their personal narratives, you're also generating completely unique content, because there is one thing that no one can replicate: real-life stories from real people. How can you start spotlighting your community?

PITCHING YOUR COLLABORATIONS

By now you should be thinking about the different approaches and ways that you can start to utilise collaborations to grow your tribe. There is one very important factor to consider when it comes to your collaborations: how you pitch them. In the same way that when you're creating content you need to ask yourself, 'what's in this for the person engaging with this?' You should be thinking the same for your collaborations: what's in it for the collaborator?

Over the years, I've worked on collaborations with big brands such as Microsoft, The Simpsons and Adobe and, as my own online community started to grow, I began to receive more requests for collaborations from brands and creators. It's safe to say I've seen a lot of pitches, emails and direct messages (DMs). It's also fair to say I know how *not* to approach someone!

I've received countless DMs saying things like, 'Hey, shall we collab? We have no budget but it's good exposure.' There are so many things wrong with this approach, but the main ones that stand out for me are: it appears as though you know nothing about me, you haven't acknowledged me or addressed why you want to collaborate with me and I may not know anything about you. And if I am happy to take 'exposure' as a value exchange, you haven't told me anything about you or your own community. Let's look at how it's done properly:

DO YOUR RESEARCH

Make sure you have carried out a full vetting process before committing to working with your collaborators. You don't want to end up working with someone and finding out further down the line that they're not the person you thought they were. This will reflect badly on you, and your community will see through this too. Remember that the people who associate with you see themselves in you – that resonance will dissipate if *you* associate with the wrong people!

MAKE IT PERSONABLE AND SPECIFIC

If you're a service provider, creator or individual looking to partner with a brand, it's so worthwhile investing some time in creating a media kit or credentials deck. I have previously used a website called pitch.com which has hundreds of templates you can use and update with your own brand elements (I've also worked with graphic designers who swear by Pitch too!). You could also look to use PowerPoint, Google Slides or any of the other design software out there (there are hundreds of them!).

Within your deck, you should look to include:

- a bio about yourself or your business
- your previous collaborations or examples of work
- your community demographic and statistics (you can pull this information from the in-app analytics across the different platforms)
- a one-pager or a few pages on the collaboration you're proposing

> (although you may want to wait until
> after you've had an initial meeting)
> • your contact details.

Always attach this so that they can get a feel for who you are and what you do.

Explain why it's them you want to partner with, reference a recent campaign or piece of content that you like and tell them why you liked it. You don't have to send them a novel in an email, but people like to know that you've researched them and you're not copying and pasting a message to everyone out there. **Make it personal.**

From experience, I've seen higher uptake in collaborations when I've sent emails. If you can't find an email address, you can always send them a DM on the platform you've found them on (although be mindful that some platforms don't allow you to message the other person if their profile is private or they don't follow you back).

I personally love LinkedIn for partnership outreach – you can find the social media manager, brand manager, partnerships manager and even creators and talent managers and go directly to the person you're trying to reach. In my opinion, no other platform facilitates professional connections in the way that LinkedIn does.

Tip: if you're reaching out to influencers (micro through to macro), UGC creators or even your customers, let them know why it's them you want to work with.

BE CLEAR ON WHAT YOU WANT

If you have a very specific idea in mind, let them know from the beginning. Also bear in mind that this is a collaboration, which means that, unless you are paying them and the agreement is that they will follow your brief, it's likely you'll also need to follow their brand guidelines and be mindful of ensuring their brand values are not compromised in any way.

(However, if you've approached your collaborations strategically, you'll be partnering with people who align with your mission anyway!)

I find having mood boards or an initial concept to expand on very helpful when pitching to brands or other creators so that they know what they are working with from the get-go.

GIVE THEM CREATIVE FREEDOM

A huge mistake I see people make is giving their partners strict and heavily scripted briefs. I've seen my favourite creators turn into robots reading from sales scripts. As consumers wise up to social media and advertising, they're looking for authentic partnerships. Your community will respect you and the person you're partnering with so much more if they can see that you've worked together to create something that feels authentic.

DON'T BE AFRAID TO FOLLOW UP

People are busy: life is filled with deadlines, notifications, dinner plans and down time. People often see emails and forget to respond. Obviously, you don't want to get your stalker 101 on and pester people – give them a reasonable amount of time – but don't be afraid to follow up, and remember that, if they say no, that's OK. It wasn't meant to be that time around, but you shouldn't eliminate the possibility for the future.

EMAIL FOOTER

Remind people in your email footer to tag you in their tutorials, videos and pictures. I've seen web designers get great coverage from the templates they sell because they constantly remind people to tag them in their new website designs on all of their email communications. Brands often put their handles at the bottom of their emails with a prompt for their communities to share their channels with their friends on social media.

Tip: you could put this in your branded newsletters and your personal email footers as a prompt to remind people to mention you in their own content, for example: 'We love to see you styling our products! Remember to tag @socialmediaprofile in your snaps to be featured on our page.'

CREATE A BRANDED

Developing a branded # is a great way to monitor your brand mentions, and anything campaign-specific too. Brands such as Chipotle do this for specific campaigns to measure the effectiveness of mentions (#boorito). I created my own branded # – #checkyourselfbeforeyournotifications – launched in line with the Mind campaign (see page 169), and use it across my wellbeing content so that I can track my mentions. Ensure that #s are short, sweet and easy to type (admittedly, mine is longer than a typical #) – the more you can eliminate potential for typos the better!

MAKE YOUR HANDLES VISIBLE

Whenever I host an event, I make sure that my handles are visible on all of my slides (handles = the names of your social media profiles, e.g. @the_self_hood). That way, if someone wants to take a photo from the event and upload it, they can see my handles. If you're a coffee-shop owner, you could print your handle on your coffee cups; if you're a designer selling prints, you could send a postcard with your handle on it; if you're a creator looking at merch, you guessed it, get your handle in there. Wherever it feels suitable, make sure you're maximising your scope for visibility so that people know exactly how to reach you.

Hopefully by now you can see that the concept of collaboration covers many areas and there are lots of ways you can collaborate with businesses, influencers, creators and even your community! When you're pitching yourself or proposing collaborations, remind yourself of how amazing you are and let that shine through in your pitch. Don't let the fear stop you from sending that email – you've got this. Now that you know how to effectively collaborate, we're going to work on creating meaningful conversations with your community and the ways you can start to nurture them with engagement-focused techniques to help you form long-lasting and powerful relationships through your content.

CHAPTER RECAP

- Make sure the people you collaborate with are in alignment with your values and conduct a vetting process first. Refer back to the collaboration-criteria diagram (see page 167) when pitching your collaborations to ensure you've covered everything.
- Start to think about how you can encourage UGC from your community.
- Use data about your community and real-life stories to bring their stories to life.
- Start working on your pitch deck to share with the people you want to collaborate with.
- When pitching your collaborations, make it personal – remember, no one likes a copy-and-paste job.

Chapter 9

COMMUNITY MANAGEMENT

'The way that I view consistency is that, yes, it's the secret to success, but it doesn't just mean posting every day. For me, consistency looks like consistently creating new connections with your audience, building relationships with your ideal community and asking them what they want. The way to consistently grow is to consistently create feedback loops.'

Grace Andrews, head of social media and content, *The Diary Of A CEO*

We've covered storytelling, finding your people, collaborations, positioning, community journeys and a whole lot more, and now it's time to dive into the hardest part of the entire process: keeping your community engaged and loyal to you.

So often people chase numbers – they want more followers, more subscribers, more fans. Because of this, they don't work on retaining their existing community and keeping them engaged. This is going to be challenging, but don't panic – I've got you. This chapter will uncover how to keep your foundations in place and reward all your hard work by ensuring your existing community stay engaged.

CREATING A SMOOTH JOURNEY

Our digital channels are very much like city breaks or road trips: every touch point and every destination is part of the journey and impacts our overall ability to reach the final destination. It also impacts how we feel about the final destination. Imagine setting off – the roof down, the sun shining and an excellent playlist for you to bob your head along to. During your journey, it pours with rain and then starts snowing. You then get a flat tyre, run out of snacks and lose signal on your phone. By the time you get to your destination, you're going to be tired and frustrated.

I want you to imagine that your website or sales call (or whatever your conversion destination is for your community) is the end point of the journey. Your social media channels, email marketing, blogs, collaborations, events, out-of-home advertising, reviews and word-of-mouth referrals are the petrol stations, the hotels, the restaurants and the coffee stops on the way.

If your touch points – aka your digital journey – aren't smooth and become stressful, this can deter your audience from ever making the visit again. They may choose a different destination and find a competitor. Your broken funnels, unlisted landing pages on your website and broken links are your flat tyre, bad weather and lack of phone signal.

Of course, we don't want this to happen – we want the digital journey to be as smooth as the movie-scene journey we picture on the highway with the 10/10 playlist and sunset to match. If your community can't find what they need, and if you're not designing external destinations with their ease of use in mind, you will lose them: fact. They will go elsewhere and your competitor will end up winning their loyalty over you – and you lose out on a Diehard Dennis for good. But, we're not about to let that happen as I'm going to share some of the ways you can start to create a harmonious journey for your community.

SYNCHRONISING YOUR COMMUNICATIONS

As we've already touched on in Chapter 1 (see page 25), consistency is key when it comes to your visuals, tone of voice and quality of content. In addition to this, it's important that your communications are aligned and that you have a consistent message, bio and handle so that you're not telling a completely different story across your platforms. Studies show that repetition increases belief, so if your brand message is different across your platforms, your story won't land with the same impact.[1]

What I'm not saying here is that your strategy can't alter – this will naturally happen. The way people communicate on LinkedIn is different to how they communicate on Twitter and hold intimate conversations on WhatsApp. That is a natural part of the process and something you will come to learn more about with ongoing observations and spending time with your community.

Ultimately, you want someone who discovers you on one platform to connect the dots as soon as they land on another. This is why it's important to treat your communications like an ecosystem that works holistically, as one, and talks to each other. I often run brand health checks with clients where we comb through communications and audit them to ensure their ecosystems align and that the brand purpose isn't being diluted due to prioritising visibility over serving the community with strong and considered content.

Tip: run brand health checks across your channels regularly to ensure your content is streamlined. A hygiene health check is ensuring that everything is consistent across your platforms and speaking the same message and language.

BUILDS FAMILIARITY

By being consistent and synchronising your communications, you'll also start to build a sense of familiarity. This is why your brand and everything we learnt in Chapter 1 is so important. Let's say I go ahead tomorrow and follow you across multiple platforms and your content looks completely different to other channels, your tone of voice is different and your purpose has changed – I may not even recognise that it's you in the first place, and all of the time and hard work you've spent creating content across different platforms becomes redundant because there is a lack of familiarity. People have very short attention spans, but by building familiarity you build trust; when you build trust, you build a community; when you build a community, more people buy from you. **The more times your brand message is heard, the better.** This is where your elevator pitch from page 00 will come in handy.

Tip: your templates and brand guidelines (see page 74) will help you remain consistent here.

GIVES YOU CREDIBILITY

Consistent messaging helps your brand feel more credible. Look at Nike's 'Just do it' for example – it has become a household phrase. Nike has been repeating its brand message across out-of-home campaigns, digital marketing, social media, TV ads and on the apparel itself. Having a consistent message across all of your channels shows your audience that you're committed to your values and helps you build credibility in your field.

KEEPS YOU FRONT OF MIND

As we know, we see up to 10,000 marketing messages per day (see page 112). Throw in two hours of scrolling, WhatsApps from friends, aggy emails, needing to do a food shop, going to the gym and a best friend's birthday gift to buy and that leaves us with a lot of information to retain and process in our day-to-day lives. Repetition of messaging and consistency across your digital channels will actually help keep you front of mind and make your brand message easier to remember.

MAKES YOUR JOURNEY HARMONIOUS

Do you have a sales, events or promotions calendar that your marketing and content can feed into? Sure, you may be using LinkedIn to promote your company culture and attract a new wave of talent and Pinterest to generate click-throughs to your products and generate sales. However, it's still crucial that your business calendar and objectives are working harmoniously across channels and that your community understands why you do what you do. You may have your Dennises over on WhatsApp and your Lindas on YouTube – they could be at different stages of their journey and migrating over platforms at different times. Ensuring that your objectives are in alignment will allow for an effortless cruise along the digital journey for your community.

LET'S TAKE THIS TO THE INBOX

Email marketing is a tactic that has been used to grow and strengthen communities for years. I've seen first-hand how email marketing impacts businesses. For many of my clients, it is still the number-one revenue-driver and the space they use to nurture their most engaged community members. It's an additional intimate space outside of the noise of social media (see page 123). With email marketing, you get direct access to your community's inbox and you're not fighting against algorithms or competition to be seen – you're there with them and have their full attention.

One thing is for sure though, email marketing is not as easy as it used to be. As consumers have become more mindful about how their data is being used, they've become more reluctant to give their information away. That's why, when you're working on your email marketing strategy, it's so important to keep asking yourself: why should they be giving you their details in exchange for access to their personal space, aka their inbox? What is the incentive?

Getting your community to migrate from social media to your website is the first task. You'll need to look at your community journey from Chapter 7 (see page 139) and address where email marketing sits within this journey before you plot it out. If you haven't started migrating your community to your mailing list, I implore you to start as soon as you can. By growing a mailing list, you're not relying on rented land and third-party platforms to speak to your tribe. Instead you're getting one-on-one access to them.

HOW TO GROW YOUR MAILING LIST
Incentives/freebies
Many product-based businesses offer email sign-up incentives, such as 10 per cent off the first order or free delivery. Many service providers offer freebies spanning from PDF worksheets to gated mini courses. It may be that incentives or offers don't align with your brand and actually what you offer them is gated and personal content that isn't available elsewhere. This is where you can really start to capture your Dennises, share longer-form content and utilise the art of storytelling to share your story in an intimate space. Remember the 80/20 rule (see page 22)? This applies for your emails too: what are you providing there that gives your community a reason to sign up?

When I was in the early stages of growing The Selfhood, I knew that I needed a space to talk to my most engaged audience. I wanted to be able to share my journey in an environment that felt contained and personal. I wanted to engage the right people – those who aligned with my values and purpose around social media and online well-being. I wrote an in-depth trend report on well-being in the online space and interviewed people in the industries I admired and included their thoughts in the report. It took me weeks to pull it together. In between client work and creating content it was a meaty task, but it generated over 700 organic downloads and secured me new bookings with brands in the wellness industry and allowed me to expand my business and outsource work to other freelancers. I also offer a bi-weekly round-up called 'What the FAQ is happening on social media' where I share interesting campaigns, resources and updates that are happening online. This content is different to the content I share on social media. I also give my newsletter list first access to new products and events, and share more personal news there.

As with any part of your digital journey, it becomes your job and your responsibility to nurture your community once they're there. The incentives and offers are merely a stepping stone to get them to your email list – you then need to be consistent with them to take them along the way.

PRODUCT-BASED BUSINESS NEWSLETTER INCENTIVE IDEAS
- Opportunities to shop new collections before anyone else
- Exclusive offers, discounts and deals
- First access to sale
- First access to behind-the-scenes content
- Interviews with the team and founder

SERVICE-BASED BUSINESS NEWSLETTER INCENTIVE IDEAS
- Trend reports
- White papers
- First access to launches and merchandise
- Gated content and resources

Discounts

Sure, discounts are a great way to drive sign-ups, but before you give anything away at a reduced rate or price, always make sure it makes sense for your margins first. It's worth noting that not everyone who signs up to your email list is guaranteed to be an OG advocate for your community – you may get some people who just want the discount (equally, you may get people who sign up and buy repeatedly and, subsequently, their purchases pay for the discount tenfold).

Ads

A great way to grow your mailing list is to run lead-generation ads. Lead-generation ads are adverts that you can run within some of the different social media platforms which allow you to collect data on the people who opt in and sign up to hear from you. You can collect data, such as name, date of birth and email address. You can then import the data you collect, upload to your mailing list and nurture them with email sequences, calls, webinars or exclusive offers and discounts (see below).

If you decide to do this, it's worth referring back to your funnel: what makes sense for your community and the service that you're offering? For example, I have previously run lead-generation ads for service providers that want to grow their online memberships. It's worth noting that something like a membership is more of a consideration piece to a Lingering Linda, as it often involves longer-term commitment and invest-ment, therefore explaining the benefits through one ad can be quite difficult and complex. With this in mind, it makes sense to showcase the membership benefits through a series of emails or alternatively a webinar where the person who is potentially signing up can find out more details and ask questions. You could also look to implement a sales call or one-to-one discovery call as part of this process depending on what you're offering.

For product-based businesses and more spontaneous purchases which don't require a huge amount of commitment or consid-eration, you could look to run a competition or offer them an exclusive incentive. For example, a restaurant could run a lead-generation ad offering the chance for someone to win brunch for themselves and three friends. Each person who opts in gets entered into a new email audience segment. They then get sent business news, offers and updates. This is a very cost-effective way to market providing that the follow-up communications are smooth and you take note of the fact that they need nurtur-ing. Remember, the same way I needed to wine and dine the lead singer of the band from page 141, your audience needs the same treatment!

Pop-ups

If you're thinking of using a pop-up on your website to grow your email list, be mindful of the user experience. Anything that is too disruptive to your website or difficult to close (particularly on mobile) can devalue your website's overall content, which can affect your organic search rankings. When adding any new updates, features or information, always be sure to test it on your mobile first. Your shiny new pop-up may work an absolute treat on a desktop, but be a royal pain in the ass for your website visitors when engaging on a mobile: test, test and test again (on multiple devices too!).

A QUICK NOTE ON GDPR

If you're based in the UK, you will need to be mindful of the General Data Protection Regulation (GDPR) – an EU law on data protection and privacy. You will also need to create a privacy policy on your website that covers how you intend to use people's data.

EMAIL SEQUENCES

Most email marketing software providers will now give you the opportunity to set up 'sequences': aka a mapped-out journey of automated emails that your audience can receive once they sign up through a specific form. I've outlined an example of this on the following page to help you understand how this could come to life:[2]

This is one top-line example, but the point is: the opportunities are endless when it comes to email marketing. You get to create intimate moments with your subscribers, give them gated content and it's a low-cost and effective way to generate interest in your business. You know that the people on your email marketing list have a warm interest in you and what you do (remember the community journey funnel exercise – see page 146).

I could follow you on TikTok, head to your Instagram account and hit 'follow'. Later on, I get served a lead-generation advert telling me about a new coffee pod you've created, offering me 10 per cent off my first purchase.

I sign up to receive the offer.

You export the data from your leads.

You add the sign-ups to a new audience segment called 'Coffee Pod New 10%'.

You could then set up a sequence and email trigger for everyone who opts in and signs up.

You send the audience an 'about us' story that introduces them to you and your business through story telling and gives them their new discount code.

Everyone who opens that email could then be sent another automated email three days later with the story and process behind how you make your coffee and your new subscription service.

You resend the original email to everyone who didn't open: research from email marketing provider Mailchimp shows that resending your email campaign to subscribers who didn't open the first time can increase your open rates by 8.7 per cent.

You could export the data from your mailing list and create a new audience to advertise to via social media ads. With this data you can also create a lookalike audience from your email subscribers. When you create a 'lookalike' audience, the advertising platforms will then create a segment of people who are from a comparable demographic and exhibit similar purchase behaviour to your OG advocates and engaged community. This is gold dust. You can go and connect with people who don't know you exist yet, but have a similar profile to those who engage with you already. Remember to think about your community journey and funnel stages when activating this – at this stage they're Lingering Lindas, but we know they have a similar profile to those who love you already; the content and incentives will need to alter based on this.

As with all of your content- and community-building techniques, email marketing requires testing. Some tests may flop and that's OK. Data isn't just there to tell us how great we are – it's there to tell us where we can improve and where we may need to up our game.

A/B TESTING

The amazing thing about email marketing is that you can run A/B tests. A/B testing is a process where you can send one email marketing message to a percentage of your email database audience and an alternative message to another. You can then gauge which has the best results and send the highest performer to the remaining people in your audience. You can A/B test pretty much everything – from your subject headers and send time, to your audience and content. A/B testing is an amazing habit for you to get into as you can start to understand patterns and trends in how your community interacts with you, and apply that data to the rest of your business. I've been working in email marketing for over 10 years and I'm still so surprised by the results we see from clients when A/B testing. Keeping track of this data is as important as testing it – without analysis, the entire task becomes redundant (look back to page 132 for more on analytics).

IRL EVENTS

As I've already mentioned, as someone who previously struggled with social anxiety, I found 'getting out there' in person very challenging at first. However, I can honestly say that one of the biggest reasons for the growth of my community and business came through attending IRL events. Had I not put myself out there, connecting with new people, there's no way I would have the opportunities, friends and connections that I have today.

So while, yes, as we've learnt throughout this book already, your digital channels are a great way to foster communities, I can't stress enough the power of IRL interactions and what they can do for your community-growth strategy.

Firstly, there's something so special about bringing your community together IRL. After overcoming my fear of public speaking through lots of practice and experiencing the magic of other people's events, I started hosting my own events for The Selfhood community and I can honestly say that meeting my community IRL has been one of my highlights since starting. Connecting in the flesh with people who had supported my social media posts, attended my webinars and who I'd chatted to online has provided some of the most special moments in my entire career. Human connection is so important; we all crave it desperately and to have the opportunity as a business owner or brand to create and facilitate those meaningful connections is an incredible privilege.

My community has gone on to tell me that they have made friends and connections through my events, both IRL and URL. Some of them have even gone on to collaborate and run their own events together! That is one of the most rewarding things about running events: seeing people come together and connecting is so special, and the good news is – you can facilitate this too.

There are lots of ways you could start to bring your community together, and don't forget that your events and in-person meetings are also an opportunity to create amazing content at the same time. Capture behind-the-scenes videos and images of your community together, and also collect live data and feedback and get them talking to each other (think about the promotional QR codes and sticker examples we spoke about in Chapter 5 – see pages 98 and 99).

You don't have to set up a full Henry VIII-style banquet and pop the champagne to serve up a good time, so please don't let the idea of this overwhelm you! Depending on your business idea, your values and your community's wants and needs, you will have your own way of connecting people. You may want to start with something like a book club, a local pizza meet-up or a co-working day in your city.

To give you some food for thought on how you could do this I've outlined some examples below:

TRAVEL BUDDIES

In 2016 home rental site Airbnb launched Airbnb Experiences as a way to bring Airbnb locals and visitors together to bond over their experiences. By syncing up hosts, travellers and members of its community, Airbnb is able to immerse its community in authenticity through their trips and experiences, bringing them together. The experiences range from meditation with Buddhist monks and cooking lessons to taxidermy lessons. There is something for everyone based on the location, but the mission is simple: to get its community to connect in person.

GLOBAL SWIM SCHOOL

Swim Dem Crew is a swimming club that was built to create a new type of swimmer: people who don't feel swimming is accessible to them but want to learn alongside like-minded people, lose their inhibitions and feel part of a community. It tours indoor and outdoor pools in London and has used its in-person swimming events to create content for its social media channels. As a result of its inspiring and heart-warming content, it's gone on to inspire other people to birth their own swimming communities overseas. By amplifying the Swim Dem mission online, it has created a highly engaged and continuously growing online and offline community.

REUSE, RENEW, RECYCLE

By Megan Crosby is a slow independent fashion brand: its values are to support the planet and create staple and iconic pieces that stand out and last a lifetime. The founder, Megan, began running workshops where the community could come along and learn how to alter old pieces of clothing. By hosting workshops that align with the By Megan Crosby ethos, the brand is reaffirming its commitment to sustainability and allowing its community to do their bit too, all while learning, meeting new people and experiencing something new.

In IRL spaces, your community will naturally gravitate towards each other because they're coming together with a common point of interest: their interest in you. It's worth noting (and this is speaking from experience), often people are nervous and introverted. When hosting my events, I try to give them prompts and icebreakers to get them talking. Many people show up to events alone and that can feel pretty overwhelming.

THINK ABOUT . . .
- How can you facilitate conversations in a way that feels organic and natural?
- Could you start with some open-ended questions?
- Weave in some creative tasks that naturally bring people together to collaborate, connect and start conversation without feeling forced.

There are many ways you can advertise your events: you could promote them through your social media channel and email list; advertise them with local press; put them on event websites such as Meetup or Eventbrite; or run sponsored ads targeted to a local audience to drive sign-ups.

When I've run events before, I've left attention-grabbing branded postcards and stickers on people's chairs with a motivational message on them that ties back to the event and The Selfhood ethos. Most people end up taking a picture of it and uploading it to their own channels and tagging me, which leads to an influx of new followers and intrigue about the event.

As we touched on in Chapter 5 (see page 79), how can you create shareable moments for your attendees to help them share your event with their own communities? Remember: peer-to-peer advocacy is one of the best ways to grow a genuine community.

Your events and meet-ups help solidify your community's love for you. They help them build bonds with you and each other and, ultimately, strengthen emotional connections, which in turn leads to greater loyalty.

COMMUNICATION IS KEY

One of the worst things businesses can do is work on amazing content, execute great ideas and produce incredible campaigns . . . and proceed to ignore and disengage with their community when they go on to show their appreciation for it.

Interacting with your community is one of, if not the, most important parts of building your social, cultural and long-term currency with your community. Remember Vicky and Michelle from Chapter 1 (see page 21)? It's important when thinking about your community management that you put your Michelle hat on: ask questions, be curious, treat your tribe like individuals and encourage them to talk to you *and* each other. If people are going out of their way to compliment your work and your content, it's up to you to acknowledge and even nurture those conversations.

THE IMPORTANCE OF THE ACKNOWLEDGEMENT

As humans, we crave to be seen and recognised for our interactions and involvement. In fact, we're hardwired to feel that way! When your community leaves comments, sends messages, interacts and engages with you, it's mostly because they're showing love and support. I always recommend allocating time each day or a few times per week to go through your messages and comments and encourage conversation or respond to them. As we spoke about with your community life cycle in Chapter 7, if someone were to compliment you or tried to engage with you in person, you wouldn't straight up ignore them, so you should be demonstrating the same etiquette online as you would in real life.

Tip: I find doing this on a desktop a lot easier than on my phone. It feels more intentional and like less of an 'admin' task and it allows me to commit and fully be present with the interactions versus being hunched over my phone.

DEALING WITH NEGATIVITY

We are all human and we can't be perfect all of the time. Social media naturally creates a space for debate and, on the rare occasion you may make a mistake or receive some negativity on your content, the best thing to do is to migrate the negativity elsewhere and be honest. I once worked with a small business that went viral unexpectedly, which led to a huge knock-on effect of late orders. We created a post to acknowledge this and apologise. We then explained that we were a small team working day and night to get the orders out. We contacted everyone who was complaining via the comments and asked them to email us directly to remove the negativity from the posts. Logistically, this is also easier for you to manage.

It's important that you have a plan in place if you ever find yourself in a social media crisis. This will allow you to act fast. There are a few things you'll need to consider:

- Create a social media policy. Make it very clear what kind of social and political issues you comment on/don't comment on and what you do and don't post.

- Have a plan for how you will communicate your crisis-response plan to your wider team. This will stop any delays in sign-off and responses from other people in the business.
- Predetermine what a crisis looks like versus an unhappy customer who can be dealt with via email.
- Pause all of your scheduled posts while you respond to ensure you deal with the issue first.
- **Don't try to hide your mistakes – always be honest. Your community will respect your transparency.**

PROVING THAT YOU'RE HUMAN

Ultimately, community management reminds your community that you're a real person. I've managed communities of over 1 million people through to my own community when it was first starting and the same thread always appears: people like to know that there is a human acknowledging them.

People are continuously pleasantly surprised to learn that there is a real person behind the platforms who is listening and responding to them. Little things like signing off your interactions with your name (if there are multiple people who are at the forefront of your business) can really help in the humanisation of your channels.

I experienced this a few years ago when my favourite beauty brand Glossier hosted a pop-up store in central London. Being the number-one fan girl I am, I went down to visit. Obviously, I took a mirror selfie, uploaded it to my own channels and tagged it in the post. Glossier responded to my tag and said, 'Thanks so much for visiting, Daisy, we hope you enjoyed it. Amelia x'

Honestly I was as star-struck as I was when I declared my love to the emo band from Chapter 7 (see page 141 for a little reminder of this traumatic humiliation). A huge business with a cult following of millions was acknowledging little old me. I was so impressed and it made me want to advocate for it more knowing that a real human was monitoring its interactions and engaging with me.

MANAGING YOUR FAN MAIL

As your business grows and your community interactions start to increase, you may need to look to hire dedicated community managers. It's important to note that this role is very different to a customer-service role. Customer service should be there to answer any support-related questions, queries and updates on your product or service specifically. Community managers are there to focus on creating engagement and relationships with your community.

There are also many tools and pieces of software you can use to respond to your community through streamlined channels in real time. A lot of the software will pull all of your social media mentions into one central space. This is super helpful, especially if you're managing a lot of interactions as you can answer them through one channel, and assign and tag different mentions depending on their requirements. If necessary, you can shoot them over to customer service for more support-related queries.

BE THE ENERGY YOU WANT TO ATTRACT

It's a well-known cultural phenomenon that great things happen in the girls' bathroom on a night out. If you're looking for an ego boost, some lipstick to borrow or a new best friend for the night, you bet it's the place to be. The girls' bathroom is filled with good energy. From the moment you walk in, you can expect an influx of compliments on your outfit and a collective singalong to a nineties dance anthem. Someone will most likely be crying about their ex and being consoled by a stranger at the same time, but it's all about girl power and that's what we're here for.

The girls' bathroom is one big energy exchange. If you acknowledge those who are in there and engage in conversation, you will be rewarded. The same principle applies to your community management. Sure, it's important to respond to the compliments and get back to those who are coming to you, but the real magic happens when you make the first move and engage with others too.

I'm connected with people on social media who don't post all of the time, but they consistently share opinions and engage with other people's content and have built engaged and loyal communities just by sharing their thoughts and opinions. **Community-building is as much about the outbound interactions as the inbound.**

Aldi is a discount supermarket chain that has garnered attention online for its punchy and relatable brand interactions across its social media channels. It often tags competitor brands in a jokey high-school rivalry way, and spends a lot of time engaging with its own community too.

Back in 2021, premium supermarket chain Marks & Spencer took legal action against Aldi alleging copyright infringement on its well-known 'Colin the Caterpillar' cake and, around the same time, Marks & Spencer made another copyright claim against Aldi relating to one of its novelty festive gins.[3]

And it turns out that supermarkets aren't the only people having beef. For years now there has been an ongoing so-called 'feud' between US singer Selena Gomez (ex-girlfriend of Justin Bieber) and model Hailey Bieber (wife of Justin Bieber) with gossip magazines and internet users globally commenting on the feud's progression. So, when a paparazzi picture of the two standing together in what appeared to be an amicable interaction went viral on Twitter, Aldi retweeted it with the caption: 'Us next @marksandspencer xxx'.[4] The tweet blew up with many praising Aldi for its humour and cheek.

Here's why the post was nothing short of iconic:

1. The interaction positioned Aldi as culturally relevant among younger demographics by hopping on a trending image featuring two of Gen Z's most prolific influencers.
2. It made the supermarket appear more human, because it wasn't taking itself too seriously.
3. It garnered lots of engagement and interaction which Aldi then went back and responded to, which in turn created actual conversation, not just casual comments.

Aldi is a great example to go and check out when it comes to brands utilising their mentions to fuel funny and interactive conversation-starters. Its tone of voice is laid back and conversational which encourages further interactions because its community knows it is constantly listening and participating. It's a win-win for both.

A great exercise for working out how you want to show up energetically is to answer this question: if your digital destinations were a physical space, how would you want people to feel? What music would you play? Would you serve food? Would it be by the beach or in a city? Would it be small and intimate or big and buzzy? Think about how you'd want your community to feel in a physical space and ask yourself if this is currently echoed online. If it's not, why not? What can you do to change this?

GO ABOVE AND BEYOND

How you show up for your community outside of social media can also translate into content and advocacy. I saw an example of this a few years ago and I'll never forget it. I was scrolling through LinkedIn and I saw a tweet someone had reposted. A woman had reached out to the pet food brand

Chewy. Her dog had sadly passed away and she had a large order she wanted to return. She relayed to her audience that Chewy had refunded her and told her to donate the food to a shelter. For me, that is one of the best business strategies we can all aspire to: providing care – care for our customers, care for our suppliers, care for the planet and care for our community.

Chewy didn't know that this customer was going to share this online. It wasn't a marketing campaign or a piece of social content – it just so happened that they did. As I've banged on throughout this book, it's about creating an experience for people beyond your product. It's about treating your community like human beings. It's an energy exchange: what energy do you want to give off?

COMMUNITY RETENTION

In my experience, retention (customers who return to your

business) is the most important part of your community management strategy, for many reasons:

- Acquiring a new community member can cost up to five times more than retaining a new one, but money isn't the only reason you should be focusing on retaining your community...
- Retention fosters genuine connection and genuine connection is what will encourage your advocates to stick around.
- Customers who repeat-buy go on to become advocates (which as we already know is one of the best ways to recruit new members into your community).

As you grow, it's inevitable you'll lose some people on the way. Community-building can be a lot like friendships – some of them come and go over the course of our lives. In fact, studies show that we replace our friends every seven years, but the ones who last and stick around for longer have been nurtured and given TLC.[5] The nature of those longer-term and unbreakable friendships holds a very different pattern to the fleeting ones – they require a level of attention, consistency and understanding. They're comprised of the following elements which can also be applied to community management:

REWARDING LOYALTY

When it comes to friendship, we acknowledge and reward our friends' loyalty in many different ways: reassuring them they weren't *that* embarrassing after too many glasses of disco juice the night before, buying them birthday gifts, telling them to stop calling their awful ex, buying a gift for their mum when they forget her birthday, picking up the bill when their card declines and, of course, giving them our most valuable commodity – our time.

Creating a loyalty and rewards programme is a great way to encourage the retention of your community. Why? Because it encourages positive reinforcement and studies show that, the more we're rewarded for our actions, the more likely we are to do it again: aka the more you reward your community, the more likely they are to stick with you.[6]

There are many loyalty programme apps and pieces of software available which you can now install across your website and integrate with your email marketing. The software allows you to monitor and prompt interaction from your community and incentivise them for their interactions spanning social media engagement, leaving reviews and sharing affiliate links, through to purchases, signing up to your newsletter and many other parameters which reward them for their commitment and loyalty to your brand. A lot of the apps now give you the freedom and flexibility to set the parameters on what your community will receive in exchange for their loyalty and it's a great way for you to start to incentivise their advocacy. This is the reason that many major global brands such as Sephora, Starbucks and The North Face use loyalty programmes. Plus the community wins too: they get extra-special treatment from their favourite brand, which gives them more reasons to shout about you and throw up the pom-poms.

As with your digital journey, your loyalty and rewards journey should be seamless and accessible. When creating your loyalty scheme it's important to consider the following factors:

Make the redemption achievable
If the rewards feel too challenging to redeem or take too long to unlock, your community will fill less compelled to finish their quest and will find something else to engage with.

Send reminders and make it visual
Studies show that when we track our progress, we're more likely to succeed in achieving our goal.[7] Therefore, keeping your community up to speed with where they're at in their rewards journey will help keep you front of mind and instil a sense of attainability. Using graphs or visuals that demonstrate their

progress will help them ascertain how far away they are from the goal and, as we discussed on page 74, we process visuals a lot faster than we do words. Most of the loyalty apps and software available offer this as a feature.

Tier your loyalty scheme
Giving your community something to aspire to will give them a boost to become more persistent in achieving the next tier, levelling them up to Diehard Dennises.

When creating your rewards scheme, it's important to think about what your community will truly want from this. It could be that you host a focus group with your most valuable community members when ideating and building your rewards scheme to develop a deeper understanding of what they truly want.

KEEPING IT FRESH
Relationships typically come to an end when we get stuck in a 'rut': we stop doing date nights, we keep wearing the old pyjamas with holes in, we stop listening to what our partner really wants and needs and, ultimately, we end up getting complacent. It's not until one day our partner ups and leaves after they've had enough of looking at the bean stains on our pyjama bottoms that we realise we should have booked the couples' cooking lessons, the pottery class or the city break to spice things up. We need new experiences to help us stay curious as curiosity improves our self-esteem and our purpose.

In the same way that staying stagnant and repeating the same patterns in our relationships will lead to disinterest, repeating the same formula and content will lead to content fatigue and a lack of engagement with your business. I see this happening all too frequently: businesses get stuck in a cycle and don't embrace new features on the social media platforms and fail to make an effort to get creative and innovative with content. It's important to remember that the digital platforms are constantly changing, as are the desires and behaviours of your community. With this in mind, it's crucial to roll with the tide and continue to monitor where you can inject some newness and creative stimulation into your strategy to keep your tribe engaged and entertained. It's also important to acknowledge this: just because a certain formula works for you right now, it doesn't mean you should keep sticking to it. How will you know where your opportunity lies if you don't continue to experiment? This all comes back to the three Cs: creativity, consistency and connection (see page 23). .

Neuroscientist Dr Duzel's research found that 'novelty' and newness trigger a release of dopamine in our brains that prompts us to stick around and learn more.[8] This is why understanding your analytics (see page 132), optimising your efforts and expanding your creative ideas is key.

BEING TRANSPARENT

In addition to complacency, many relationships fail due to lack of communication, accountability and awareness of our own actions. As humans, we're attracted to self-awareness, honesty and transparency; we're drawn to those who not only recognise their faults but own up to them and go on to work on them. The same goes for businesses. According to research conducted by *Forbes*, over 90 per cent of consumers say transparency in a brand is important to their purchase decisions.[9] Typically, we're more inclined to stick around and support the businesses that are committed to doing better: the ones that listen to feedback, implement it and tell us how they are doing so.

It may be that you're investing in new packaging or materials, hiring new members of your team, investing in better software or adding new skills to the business to improve the overall customer experience. It's important to acknowledge that, if you decide to share these updates, it should never be performative – you should only share if it is genuine and benefits your community. This is by no means an opportunity to showboat and you absolutely must be able to back your claims of improvements with evidence. If not, your community will go looking for them.

It's also important to note that it's OK to acknowledge that you're not perfect, but you're working on it. A great example of utilising feedback to improve is the IKEA Co-Creation concept (see page 18). By speaking directly to its community and understanding where it can improve, IKEA is able to develop a product that meets its community's needs.

STAYING CONNECTED

When we meet our friends and family for coffee, pick up the phone or send voice notes or DMs, the premise is that we're usually checking in and asking each other about the updates and progressions in our lives: 'Did you get the promotion?' 'How're your studies?' 'Did you get a second date?' 'Did your mum's surgery go well?'

We want to know what's happening in each other's worlds because it makes us feel part of each other's lives. Your community wants to know what you're up to because it helps them build a deepened connection with you. That's why the segment on behind-the-scenes content and brand-building content is a crucial part of your community-management strategy (see page 120).

FUTURE-PROOFING YOUR BUSINESS

Throughout this book we've uncovered what it takes to create a unique brand story and share it online, craft your values, identify who sits within your own community, how to effectively collaborate, create processes, form a community journey, retain your community and a whole lot more. It's important to think about how to future-proof your business too, as social media changes so frequently. We covered advertising changes and restrictions on tracking on page 124 and the importance of growing your mailing list on page 193 because I want you to be aware of these changes and think about how you can set yourself up for success with this in mind.

I've recapped some of the key points that we've covered below as this is going to help you when it comes to longevity and future success for your business:

- Strive for advocacy: the most effective way to grow a successful business with a long-lasting legacy is through growing a community that proudly advocates for you. I want you to strive for Diehard Dennises. Listen to your community, create an incredible experience at every touch point and go above; they will then stay loyal to you.
- Ask for constant feedback: without staying in close contact with your community you won't know how they feel about you now and, worse yet, what they expect from you in the future. Staying ahead of the curve when it comes to serving them is key to a fruitful future.
- Grow your owned data: remember owned data includes email addresses, phone numbers, app installs and postal addresses. I've said it once and I'll say it again: social media is rented land. If the platforms went bust tomorrow, it's so important you have intimate spaces to connect with them in (see page 123 for a refresher on this).
- Network: growing an online community is amazing, and the visibility and reach online is incredible! But, as we know from page 54, networking is vital for building key relationships and a strong web of people who can help you.

Please don't sleep on community management! Admittedly, this part of community-building can get put on the back burner and be an afterthought, particularly when things get busy, but the rewards and benefits are so key. Remember in Chapter 1, when we spoke about the difference between an audience and a community (see page 14)? Working on a strong community-management strategy is one of the best ways to migrate from audience to community.

Next up we're going to talk about bringing all of our ideas together through creative thinking and mindset towards social media. This is going to help you boost your confidence and put all of the groundwork we've been through together straight into action.

CHAPTER RECAP

- Check your message is consistent across your channels:
- Does your website tell the same story as your social media channels?
- Do your social media channels tell the same story as your newsletter?
- Invest in a data-capture strategy. How can you work on growing your mailing list so that you're not solely focusing on third-party apps to communicate with your audience? What incentives will you offer?
- Start thinking about how you could connect with your community offline too.
- Make time to work on your inbound and outbound strategy. Open your laptop and respond to your interactions each week. Allocate time to reach out to potential community members too.
- How can you encourage your community to stick around by incentivising them?
- Showcase your business updates, improvements and keep your content fresh and exciting to keep your community engaged and stimulated.

Chapter 10

KEEP YOUR CREATIVE JUICES FLOWING

'One day you'll get to my age, 85, and you'll not give a damn about what anyone else thinks and wish you could do it all again.'

Anne Gibbins, TikTok fanatic and my nan

Growing a community isn't always sunshine and roses. There are times when you may struggle to put yourself out there or feel like your content is 'flopping'. You'll ebb in and out of your groove and I want you to know that feeling this way is so normal. The rollercoaster ride can often have a knock-on effect when it comes to our creativity and ability to come up with ideas for our community. In this chapter, we're going to cover how to stay motivated and creative when you're struggling with being visible and when negative self-talk Tina pops up (see page 63) and you feel like throwing in the towel.

THE PERILS OF CREATIVE BURNOUT

In 2020 my business grew very quickly and, if I'm totally honest, I wasn't ready for it. As lots of businesses pivoted throughout the Covid-19 pandemic to focus on their online sales and marketing, the demand for social media and digital marketing sky-rocketed. I suddenly went from being a contracted freelancer to a fully booked business owner with a waiting list. On top of ideating content ideas, marketing strategies, creating content and pulling reports for clients, I was also working on admin, finance, marketing, sales, discovery calls, proposals and managing a small team for my own business.

After six months of 7am starts and 12am finishes I became totally and utterly burnt out to the point that my hair started to fall out and I was having severe heart palpitations. In today's society, the phrase 'burnout' has become a bit of a buzzword and, in many ways, a very sad symbolic badge of honour – a signal to our peers that we're dedicating so much to our work that our bodies and minds have failed us.

Not only was my physical health suffering, my mind was all over the place too. I couldn't think straight, I had severe creative block and I felt totally fatigued and out of things to talk about. It was as if my creative tank had run out of petrol – aka creative juices – and I was left feeling like a total zombie.

I found it hard to hold a conversation with my nearest and dearest, let alone think about big ideas and conceptualise content for myself and clients. I felt so unwell that I couldn't interact with my own community and ended up resisting social media altogether. It had completely broken me and the thought of opening my apps filled me with dread.

In the end, I was told to take time off by my doctor and I took some time away from work and caught my breath for a while. I want to stress here that I am not proud of letting that happen. In fact, for a long time, I felt incredibly unhappy and embarrassed about the state I'd allowed myself to get into and I absolutely do not advocate for overworking. The reason I'm choosing to share this is because there was a big lesson in the health challenges I faced and I truly believe that there is always a breakthrough on the other side of the breakdown.

During my recovery, I spent time away from work and read books and listened to podcasts. I remembered what it was like to laugh again at comedy nights; I learnt new perspectives at open-mic nights; and filled my brain with colour at art galleries. I refilled my empty and rusty tank with creativity. By stepping away from the pressure of being a constant creative generator, I gave myself time to get excited by resources, experiences and connections that took place outside of my phone. The juice was flowing again and so were my ideas. I felt more creative than ever. I had the most incredible conversations with my community and it was flourishing faster than I had ever thought possible because I was bringing good energy back to the conversation.

Nurturing a community takes time and, with time, come many ebbs and flows. From putting yourself out there to the world, doubting your value, the content not always landing, wanting to pack it all up, throw your phone in the bin and become a tree surgeon instead, to then doing a full 180 and finding your flow and realising your magic. A lot of the ebbs will come from how aligned you feel with not only your purpose and your work, but also yourself. Please don't eye-roll, hear me out: I know that sounds very 'woo-woo', but, as we already know, community-building is an energy exchange. If your cup isn't full and you're not taking time for you, your content will feel rushed, panicked and stagnant.

THE REALITIES OF BUILDING AN ONLINE COMMUNITY

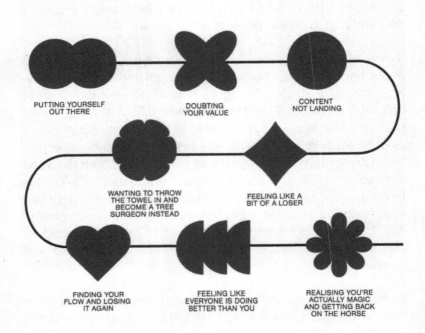

PUTTING YOURSELF OUT THERE

DOUBTING YOUR VALUE

CONTENT NOT LANDING

WANTING TO THROW THE TOWEL IN AND BECOME A TREE SURGEON INSTEAD

FEELING LIKE A BIT OF A LOSER

FINDING YOUR FLOW AND LOSING IT AGAIN

FEELING LIKE EVERYONE IS DOING BETTER THAN YOU

REALISING YOU'RE ACTUALLY MAGIC AND GETTING BACK ON THE HORSE

MAKE THE JUICE WORTH THE SQUEEZE

When I got out the other side of my burnout experience, I started to ponder what had gone wrong. I monitored my work habits and started to track where the catalysts were for stress and overworking. Throughout this process, I created a concept on creative juices, and I want to share it with you because it's going to impact your content creation and how you can bring creativity and 100 per cent of your energy to your community.

100 PER CENT ORGANIC SQUEEZED ORANGE JUICE

This is the juice that we make from real-life interactions and observations: **the conversations we have with real people; the textures we admire on a painting; the breakdown in your favourite song when it is played differently at a live show; the poem that gives you goosebumps at an open-mic night; the embarrassing story your best mate tells you at dinner that makes you cry with laughter; and that smile you exchange with a cute stranger on the train that lasts longer than normal.** These are all little moments that bring us presence and let our brains run wild for a second. These are the moments that allow us to think, the ones that truly allow us to use our imagination. The real, raw, unprocessed juice comes from organic interactions and sparks a unique idea or feeling in you.

ORANGE CORDIAL

This is the watered-down 'fake' juice we fill our tanks with after embarking on a doomscroll session and the overconsumption of other people's content. The longer you scroll for, the more diluted the juice becomes.

When we consume more than we create, we're temporarily quenching our thirst, but after a while we're going to regret not going for the real deal. When we rely solely on others' content, we're filling our inspo tank with recycled goods.

Now, I'm all about a balanced lifestyle and often partake in a little thirst-quenching. It's also good to have an understanding of what's happening online and stay up to date with changes in your community's habits and engagement patterns. Plus, as we discussed in Chapter 4, it's great to keep up to speed on what's happening in your industry (see page 66).

But the real innovation and original thinking comes from the freshly squeezed oranges. It's important to strike a balance and make sure that you're seeking inspiration outside of your social media feeds too. Not just for your content, but for your mental health. Overconsumption and drinking too much cordial can also catapult us into comparisonitis (see page 63) and spiral us into negative thoughts – and that will ultimately lead to posting paralysis and stop us from getting the magic out there altogether.

You might be thinking: what's all this juice chat got to do with my community-building strategy? Well, have you ever gone to a social event that you really didn't want to go to? You were so tired and just wanted to stay at home and watch Netflix but you dragged yourself there anyway and ended up keeping quiet and leaving early? The same flat 'I-don't-really-want-to-be-here' energy that we give off when we're at the social event we really don't want to be at translates online too: when you show up to the party without really wanting to be there, your community will sense it; when you post to tick the box they'll know. It's better to take some time out to fill your cup and go to the party when you've got the energy to bring the heat on the dance floor. As we saw in the last chapter with the girls' bathroom: *everything is energy*. When we have a full cup of the 100 per cent organic squeezed orange juice, we can give our communities the best of us and serve them the good stuff too.

CREATIVE THINKING TIME

'Creative thinking time' is now a key component in my content creation process. Whether it's content that I create for my Selfhood community or campaigns I work on for clients, you best believe that creative thinking time is going into the project timeline. It's an absolute non-negotiable and one I implore you to embed into your own process too. Creative thinking time doesn't always have to mean going to gigs, galleries or leaving the country for headspace – there are other ways you can think creatively that cost little to no money:

LEAVE YOUR HOUSE WITHOUT HEADPHONES AND GO SOMEWHERE, ANYWHERE

I learnt this lesson a few years ago when I was running late to get to the airport and, when I arrived, I realised I had forgotten my beloved headphones. I was so late I had to run through customs to catch my flight and didn't have time to pick up new headphones or a book. The flight wasn't long enough to screen films, so I did something which could be considered wild in the modern-day world – I sat in silence and observed. This sounds extremely dramatic, but that journey was one of the most pivotal moments of my life. I had some of the biggest and most profound personal and professional realisations. I now frequently make journeys without digital distractions and it is game changing for conceiving and growing ideas.

Tip: leave a small symbolic sticker on your headphone case to help you break up with them. Every time you look at the sticker you'll be reminded to question whether you *really* need them.

GO FOR A WALK OR CHANGE YOUR SCENERY

A Stanford study found that walking increases creative output by 60 per cent and movement allows ideas to flow more freely.[1] Within the study, 100 per cent of those who walked outside were able to generate at least one high-quality, novel analogy compared to 50 per cent of those seated inside. Professor Kimberly Elsbach, who studies workplace psychology, found that, 'staying inside, in the same location, is really detrimental to creative thinking. It's also detrimental to doing that rumination that's needed for ideas to percolate and gestate and allow a person to arrive at an "aha" moment.'[2] Getting outside and experiencing a natural environment, even for a few minutes, is restorative.

If you're unable to go for a walk, simply changing your routine and scenery can do wonders for your creative juices. Changing the scenery forces our brains to adapt to new surroundings and therefore think differently. It gets us out of a cyclical and repetitive mindset that could potentially halt us from thinking outside of the box.

Tip: schedule in a creative walk (even if it's just to the shop to get a snack of choice). If you're unable to get outside to walk, make time to work from a new café or space as part of your weekly routine.

TALK IT OUT

We're often told to stay quiet about our ideas and keep them to ourselves and I call BS on this. Through networking and community-building, I've built a network of friends who I meet with regularly to talk big dreams, plans and content ideas. Talking to others about your ideas helps you bring a fresh perspective, and verbalising your thoughts can help you come to decisions and elevate your concepts. Finding people you can trust to give you honest and constructive feedback will help you to advance your ideas.

Tip: find an accountability partner in your community, at work or among your friendship group to talk your ideas out with. Ensure that time is dedicated to ideation only so that it feels more intentional.

TAKE A SHOWER OR HAVE A BATH

This one isn't a direct insult, just a suggestion. I once heard a story about a CEO who had a shower installed in their office. Every time they were stuck on a solution or idea they'd take a shower and the answer would come. Why? Because it's one of the few times throughout our day when we take intentional time to think with zero distractions or notifications.

Tip: wash – as much as possible.

LET IT MARINATE

Allow your idea time to evolve naturally. Plant the seed and let it shapeshift and grow into something unexpected. Allow it to naturally expand and form into something new.

Tip: schedule in your creative thinking time to plant your seeds and book in additional time to revisit at a later date and see how your ideas have evolved since your initial spark.

SEEK INSPIRATION OUTSIDE OF YOUR INDUSTRY

It's easy to look at 'sexy' brands in the creative industry to see how they're marketing themselves and working on growing a community. As we discussed in Chapter 5, seeking inspiration in less obvious places and finding businesses and sectors that have a tougher time creating 'fun' content will be highly beneficial when looking to get inspired. Sticking to your industry alone will stagnate your creativity so be sure to branch out far and wide.

Tip: make a list of industries you feel would have a tough time creating innovative and creative content and go and look at what some of the content trailblazers are doing.

If all else fails, abort the task altogether. Move on to something else – don't force it.

SHOWING UP

'Showing up' is a phrase that was coined by Woody Allen when he said, '80 per cent of life is just "showing up".'[3] Showing up means putting in effort. It has now become widespread internet slang for 'being present online' and, more commonly, 'showing your face and being visible within your brand or business'. This is something that many people struggle with and I am not going to sit here and say that it's easy because I understand that it's not. For many of us it can trigger body-image issues and inflame insecurities, as we analyse every detail of how we look and sound. This can go on to stunt our creativity – we spend so much time overanalysing how we appear online and end up questioning ourselves due to fear of judgement, that we end up holding back on our ideas and big vision. I want to share some of the ways in which I overcame this myself in the hope that I can inspire some courage in you too.

As I've already mentioned, public speaking used to be my biggest fear. Every time I had to present or talk I would feel as though the world was crashing down around me. The first video I ever posted on my social media accounts was like watching an episode of *Robot Wars*, except the robot was wearing a brown curly wig . . . the robot was me. I was stiff and bright red and it took me an entire day to film a 30-second clip.

Now, I create content daily. I'm comfortable with filming myself and I even get paid to do public speaking for brands and conferences. If you'd have told me this a few years ago, I'd have spat out my coffee and told you to get lost. I don't share this to gloat – I just want you to know that it can be scary and it's not a natural or easy thing to do initially, but I want you to get comfortable with this because speaking with confidence and feeling good about how you show up on camera will impact how you can serve your own community.

Hopefully by now you understand the benefits of humanising your brand and the impact that this will have on growing your community and building a business that feels real and genuine, so I'm not going to go on about that. What I will say is having real people at the forefront of your business is really going to help you build familiarity and trust with your community. The tips I've outlined below are relevant for both in-person public speaking and talking to the camera, so if you feel like you've mastered talking to the camera and creating content, but you'd rather go into work naked than talk to a room full of hundreds of strangers, this part is for you.

GET COMFORTABLE WITH YOUR VOICE
If you're one of the many people in the world who cringe at the sound of your own voice, then come on in and join the club. The first time I listened back to my voice after recording content I

gave myself the full-blown ick. In my head, my voice sounded like a cross between Gemma Collins and a crying cat. It put me off creating content, but I knew I had to do it. Plus, spending time worrying about minor details is wasted energy that could be spent creating valuable content for my community. I listened back to my voice notes to friends, recorded myself on Zoom calls and then started to pitch myself on podcasts. Over time, I grew familiar with my voice and embraced it – I even went on to create a podcast called *That Feeling When* ... with my two friends Stef Sword-Williams and Poonam Dhuffer.

It's worth noting that recordings sound different to the voice we're used to hearing when speaking. This is due to the physiology of our skulls making our voices sound deeper when we talk and therefore more high-pitched when we hear them back via recordings. Essentially, we feel shocked hearing our own voices because we're simply not used to it. I would highly recommend spending some time recording yourself and listening back to familiarise yourself with how you sound. Yes, it's cringe, but I promise it will help.

PRACTISE
I've divulged a lot of embarrassing things in this book and this is probably up there with one of the most 'cringeworthy', but, here goes: I often walk down the street with headphones in and rehearse my pitches, workshops and talks out loud because people just assume I'm on the phone (and also everyone is the main character in their own lives so why on earth would they care about what I'm talking about on an average Tuesday at 4pm?).

Practising talking about your topic out loud and in your own rhythm and flow will help you when it comes to 'showing up' on camera or pitching yourself for podcasts and interviews. Of course, you don't have to walk down the road with headphones in; you could do this from the comfort of your own home or practise your topics with friends or alone into the camera. I personally like the walking method because, as we've just discussed on page 223, walking sparks creativity and I often find my ideas and thoughts flow easier and often expand and marinate as I'm walking.

Putting in a bit of practice will also boost your confidence. You can iron out any points that you struggle to verbalise and pay extra attention to that topic. You'll also start to identify the ideas that you feel super confident speaking about and can hone in on those when you're starting out or pitching your ideas to others.

MICRODOSE YOUR CONFIDENCE

In recent years 'microdosing' has become a popular practice in the wellness industry – it's the concept of administering a very small amount of a drug (mostly psychedelics) in order to improve mental health. A few years ago I started microdosing myself – not on magic mushrooms or LSD, but on confidence.

I identified what was holding me back from really 'showing up'. I got honest with myself and looked at my triggers. What I found while introspecting was that I had an inferiority complex that was preventing me from talking about my work and business confidently. I felt like a fraud and would spiral into comparisonitis every time I looked at what my competitors were doing. This also showed up at networking events – everyone would have their amazing elevator pitches and I really struggled to 'own it'.

Now, a lot of 'tech bro' podcasts will tell you to fight the fear and do it anyway, to dive straight into the deep end and 'put yourself out there'. I found that diving head-first into the networking world didn't work for me. I once felt so uncomfortable that I asked a man at a professional networking event what animal he would be and why because I didn't know what else to say. He was as confused as I was and I left very shortly after, although in case you were wondering he did answer (I think it was out of pity) and he said a dog because they're friendly and full of energy. It was a strange encounter, to be honest, but he spared me a small piece of humiliation, so I'm grateful for that.

After realising that my inferiority complex was stopping me from serving my community and sharing the things I loved to talk about, I knew I needed to gradually build myself up over time. Each week I would set myself small and measurable tasks that would boost my confidence. I started off by pushing myself to talk to strangers. I would ask baristas, bus drivers and cashiers how their day was going or if they had plans after work. I'll be honest, a few times I think people thought I was either drunk or coming on to them because I live in east London which is notoriously busy and not as conversational as other parts of the world, but it got me out of my comfort zone and familiar with the idea of talking to strangers.

Once I got comfortable making small talk, I pitched myself to speak on other people's podcasts. I could do that from the comfort of my own home in my tracksuit and it felt less confronting than talking to a room full of strangers.

I then hosted my own virtual workshop to my community, then spoke as a guest speaker on panels and eventually plucked up enough courage to host an IRL community workshop which sold out in a matter of hours. All of this took time, practice and patience. It was not an overnight thing.

The microdosing rule applies to any part of your life that you're struggling with, whether it's speaking up in meetings or building yourself up to a solo travel trip by taking yourself to the cinema or dinner alone – whatever you need to work on.

It's like the rewards scheme we spoke about in the last chapter: making your actions achievable will send off reward signals to your brain and make you want to unlock the next level or, in this case, your next dose of confidence.

JEDI (JUST EFFING DO IT)
Sigh I know, you're going to hate me for this, and this is the advice that no one ever wants to hear (including me), but sadly it's the pill we all need to swallow so I'm just going to say it: just effing do it. Pick up the camera, the microphone, the iPhone, the

webcam – however you want to get this show started – and try. Even if no one sees it, even if you don't post it, try. And then try again. And again. And when you're at least 50 per cent OK with it, get it out there because you're never going to love it at first, but your community won't care about the details you're sweating over.

Remember this: **the only thing you can guarantee by not posting that piece of content is that your idea won't take off**. Whether you're uploading your first podcast episode, starting the get-ready-with-me vlog, sharing your new products or getting your ideas out there, you can't be sure whether anyone will engage with your content if you don't put it out there. Equally, you can't know whether you'll get a positive or negative response if it doesn't exist for anyone to see.

What you can guarantee is that no one will ever know about it and your dream is still an idea because it's sitting in the notes section on your phone and not on your profiles. There, I said it.

I've worked on campaigns with huge influencers, celebrities and full-time presenters and the truth is: they still get nervous about showing up too. They still mess up their lines, have to repeat the script or get completely tongue-tied, but we only see the glossy end product. If this is something that you struggle with, please know that you're not alone. I've found that being honest and transparent with my community helps. I'll say, 'I feel quite nervous about this' or 'I'm struggling to get my words out today' – they understand that I'm only human. Besides, we all love a blooper, right?

DON'T LET THE TROLLS GET YOU DOWN

I want to share this anecdote about something I experienced early on in my journey because it's something that others have told me they fear countless times, and there are a few big lessons in the experience. After six months of consistently post-ing, I became comfortable with posting content and I was getting good at being consistent with providing value and education for my community. I was posting regular video content and getting a great response – this was reflected in my newsletter sign-ups too. I would get messages from my community telling me that they had recommended my resources to their friends and even had a few members of my community recognise me on my coffee runs! I couldn't quite believe that my socially anxious, awkward self had managed to break through my fears and bring people together to connect over the thing that I loved to talk about most.

One day I woke up ready to go to work and saw what every person putting themselves out there on social media fears: a troll. Someone had taken it upon themselves to spam my posts with comments such as 'cringe' and a now personal favourite, 'geek pie'. I want to caveat here that I'm fully aware that many creators and people who put themselves out there encounter far worse trolling than this, especially those from marginalised communities, and I am in no way equating my own experience to theirs. However, I still want to share how I navigated this in the hope that it may help you overcome any doubts in your confidence (which is totally normal, by the way!).

It still hurts to read this as someone who had worked really hard to build their own confidence. I remember feeling flustered and going through my posts and indoctrinating myself with negative thoughts: 'maybe I am a geek', 'what if I am really cringe?' 'I wonder if my friends all laugh at me behind my back'. I stopped posting for a few days and honestly questioned whether to delete my social media accounts. I know that sounds dramatic, but it really hurt my confidence.

Throughout that time, I confided in a few friends. I was sitting in the pub and one of them said something to me that I always come back to and want to share here, and as Eleanor Roosevelt once said: **'no one can make you feel inferior without your consent'**. I had allowed user8764527 with no profile picture hiding behind a troll account to make me feel unworthy. I had chosen to focus on the one negative comment among the hundreds of words of support and encouragement. Instead of focusing on the people who may not like what you do – whether it's your disapproving old-fashioned grandma, your boss or a stranger on the internet, there will always be someone who doesn't vibe with what you do and that's a good thing – focus on the great things that people say about you. It's better to be loved by a solid community of 100 people than have 1,000 people sitting on the fence.

When you start to spiral into self-doubt or think about what people might say about you, you have to remember the facts. When your brain starts telling you 'people are laughing at me behind my back' or 'my community are sick of me', you have to ask: how do I know this? Where is the evidence? Our brains are extremely clever and will have us up all night thinking all sorts. Always remember to double F yourself and ask: fact or fiction? Having confidence in your ideas allows you to become more expansive in your thoughts. When you're not worrying about what other people think or sweating over the minor details, like whether your hair looks a bit frizzy and your nails could do with some love, you allow yourself to create from a full space that feels aligned and free.

Creativity can't be forced – it takes time and patience. In a world that often demands us to be 'always on' and constantly innovating, it's so important that you take the time to fill your own cup with the freshly squeezed orange juice. To grow the orange, you have to plant the seed (idea), water the soil, nurture it and let it grow. Give yourself permission to think. When you allow your creativity to shine, you naturally feel more confident in your work. I really want you to remember to give yourself permission to step away from your screen and indulge (guilt-free) in whatever allows you to switch off and be present. That is when the magic happens.

CHAPTER RECAP

- Make sure that you're scheduling in creative thinking time as part of your ideation process. Look for inspiration outside of your screens.
- Switch up your environment and your routine – it will do wonders for your creativity.
- Confidence doesn't happen overnight. Work on small steps and build yourself up. Set small and measurable tasks and up the ante when you get comfortable.

FINAL NOTE

I want to end the book on this note: whether you want to become the next YouTube sensation, create a podcast for reptile enthusiasts or start a Discord community for astrology fans, it is your right to go and get what you want. When you take the initial plunge, when you start to share your passions or think of ideas that may be a little out of the box, it's easy to roll back and start ruminating over that thing that someone once said to you in 1998 or panic that your team or your boss will think the ideas are shit. When those thoughts start to creep in, always remember the people you're helping.

This has been my saving grace when I've thought about throwing in the towel and doing something else, when I've questioned whether my content – and even myself – is relevant. Remember your community and the impact you're making.

As well as thinking back to the people you're helping, be sure to track your progress and your wins. I have a WhatsApp group with two of my friends Stef and Poonam. Each week we send in our 'wins before dins' and share what we've achieved that week. It could be anything from going for a walk twice that week, sending off a scary proposal, having a sticky conversation, or waking up early enough to get to the gym, but you do need to make sure that you're keeping track of the great things you're doing.

Sharing your work, finding the courage to start a business and take that leap is unbelievably courageous. Having to then promote it online and grow a community can feel extremely exposing and, as Brené Brown once said, it can leave us with a 'vulnerability hangover'.[1] The honest truth that I've come to understand while enduring my vulnerability hangovers is that anyone who has a problem with you showing up as yourself, putting yourself out there and trying to do well for yourself is always projecting their own insecurities onto you. They're not the people for you, and that's OK. There are thousands of people out there waiting to join your community and connect with you and your magic, and I'm so excited for you. So go on then – go get 'em.

ACKNOWLEDGEMENTS

There are so many people I would love to thank for guiding me along this journey. There are too many to list here, however, in particular, I want to thank my friends and family who have supported me and helped me along the rollercoaster and reminded me I could push through the difficult times, even when I thought I couldn't. This book wouldn't have been possible without you.

To the incredible team at Yellow Kite for believing in me. Holly Whitaker: although you're no longer with the company, you have been an instrumental part of this journey. I'm so grateful that you saw something in me and The Selfhood and gave me the chance to become a published author. To Carolyn Thorne and Julia Kellaway for reassuring me when the negative self-talk popped up – you guided me through the imposter syndrome and I'm so thankful for your words of wisdom.

To Ryan, for being my cheerleader and reminding me of my sparkle when I couldn't find it – you have the patience of a saint. I don't know where I'd be without you being there through the hard times.

To Sinead Taylor for bringing The Selfhood visuals to life and understanding my vision every single time. The Selfhood would not be the same without you.

To every single person who contributed to this book: Tasha, Ellie, Jasmine, Peigh, Rachel, Amber, Nadī-Samia, Ellijah, Grace and my nan. Your contributions and the work you do professionally and for your communities have inspired me in so many ways.

To Poonam and Stef, my work wives, agony aunts and forever inspirations. You helped me nurture my creativity and bring The Selfhood to life from the very beginning.

To my art teacher, Mr Matthews, for helping me find my own selfhood and share it with the rest of the world, and to my

English teacher Miss Salmon, who told me I would never pass my English exam: I hope you enjoy the book.

And finally, to every single person who has ever shared my posts, told their mates about The Selfhood at the pub, recommended it to a friend, attended my events and supported my work – you are my community and I wholeheartedly mean it when I say none of this would be possible without you.

ENDNOTES

CHAPTER 1: THE IMPORTANCE OF COMMUNITY

1 Bonner, M., 29 May 2019. An influencer with 2 million followers couldn't sell 36 T-shirts and Twitter is NOT OKAY. *Cosmopolitan*. Retrieved from https://www.cosmopolitan.com/entertainment/celebs/a27623334/influencer-arii-36-shirts-2-million-followers/.

2 IKEA, n.d. Co-creation. Retrieved from https://about.ikea.com/en/life-at-home/co-creation.

3 Fair Play Talks, 22 Dec. 2021. 6/10 consumers want to shop with brands treating staff well. Retrieved from https://www.fairplaytalks.com/2021/12/22/6-10-consumers-want-to-shop-with-brands-that-treat-staff-well-study-reveals/.

CHAPTER 2: KNOW WHAT YOU STAND FOR

1 Aziz, A., 17 Jun. 2020. Global study reveals consumers are four to six times more likely to purchase, protect and champion purpose-driven companies. *Forbes*. Retrieved from https://www.forbes.com/sites/afdhelaziz/2020/06/17/global-study-reveals-consumers-are-four-to-six-times-more-likely-to-purchase-protect-and-champion-purpose-driven-companies/?sh=3636e112435f.

2 Ahmed, A., 20 Jul. 2022. Twitter and Publicis conduct research on how social media discourse affects brand and product sales. Digital Information World. Retrieved from https://www.digitalinformationworld.com/2022/07/twitter-and-publicis-conduct-research.html.

3 The Diary Of A CEO, 9 Jun. 2022. The marketing genius behind Nike: Greg Hoffman [podcast]. YouTube. Retrieved from https://www.youtube.com/watch?v=nWwnm-z6m0w.

4 Havas Media Group, 21 Feb. 2019. Building meaningful is good for business: 77% of customers buy brands who share their values. Retrieved from https://havasmediagroup.com/building-meaningful-is-good-for-business-77-of-consumers-buy-brands-who-share-their-values/#:~:text=Havas%20Market-,Building%20meaningful%20is%20good%20for%20business%3A%2077%25%20of.%20consumers%20buy,brands%20who%20share%20their%20values&text=A%20massive%2077%25%20of%20brands,and%20no%2Done%20would%20care.

5 Dodgson, L., 5 Jan. 2017. Getting emotional might actually help us remember things, not make us forget them. *Insider*. Retrieved from https://www.businessinsider.com/emotions-improve-memory-2017-1?r=US&IR=T.

6 Goodreads, n.d. Maya Angelou quotes. Retrieved from https://www.goodreads.com/quotes/5934-i-ve-learned-that-people-will-forget-what-you-said-people.

7 @ashaunnakayars, Jan. 22. Someone once asked me to describe my brand ... Instagram. Retrieved from https://www.instagram.com/p/Cns2ZXtrRMp/?hl=en.

8 Pillen, K., 25 Feb. 2022. Can you really fall in love with anyone? TrendsActive. Retrieved from https://www.trendsactive.com/2022/02/25/can-you-really-fall-in-love-with-anyone/.

CHAPTER 3: FIND YOUR PEOPLE

1 Butler, S., 9 Dec. 2012. Fresh, but not so easy: Tesco joins a long list of British failure in America. *Guardian*. Retrieved from https://www.theguardian.com/business/2012/dec/09/fresh-not-easy-tesco-british-failure-america.

2 Horizon Media, 3 Oct. 2022. Marketing to Gen Z: Subcultures are the new demographics. *PR Newswire*. Retrieved from https://www.prnewswire.com/news-releases/marketing-to-gen-z-subcultures-are-the-new-demographics-301639134.html.

CHAPTER 4: MAKE YOUR MARK

1 @KimKardashian, 3 Dec. 2021. They can steal your recipe ... [tweet]. Twitter. Retrieved from https://twitter.com/KimKardashian/status/1466766638519177217.

2 Twitter, 10 Mar. 2014. What fuels a Tweet's engagement? [blog]. Retrieved from https://blog.twitter.com/en_us/a/2014/what-fuels-a-tweets-engagement.

3 Sibley, A., 3 Feb. 2017. 19 reasons you should include visual content in your marketing [blog]. HubSpot. Retrieved from https://blog.hubspot.com/blog/tabid/6307/bid/33423/19-reasons-you-should-include-visual-content-in-your-marketing-data.aspx.

CHAPTER 5: SHARE YOUR MAGIC

1 Dixon, S., 14 Feb. 2023. Global social networks ranked by number of users 2023. Statista. Retrieved from https://www.statista.com/statistics/272014/global-social-networks-ranked-by-number-of-users/.

2 Shepherd, J., 3 Jan. 2023. 22 essential Twitter statistics you need to know in 2023. Social Shepherd. Retrieved from https://thesocialshepherd.com/blog/twitter-statistics.

3 Creative Review, n.d. Nike (1987) – Just do it. Retrieved from https://www.creativereview.co.uk/just-do-it-slogan/#:~:text=Considering%20how%20intrinsic%20to%20the,training%2C%20basketball%20and%20women's%20fitness.

4 Vividfish, 13 Sep. 2017. 75% of customers say they use social media as part of the buying process. Retrieved from https://www.vividfish.co.uk/blog/75-of-customers-say-they-use-social-media-as-part-of-the-buying-process.

CHAPTER 6: THE CONTENT CREATION PROCESS

1 Simpson, J., 25 Aug. 2017. Finding brand success in the digital world. *Forbes*. Retrieved from https://www.forbes.com/sites/forbesagen-cycouncil/2017/08/25/finding-brand-success-in-the-digital-world/?sh=ea124dd626e2.

2 Adams, P., 19 Oct. 2022. Pepsi CMO on state of media fragmentation: 'A double-edged sword'. Marketing Dive. Retrieved from https://www.marketingdive.com/news/pepsi-cmo-media-fragmentation-tiktok-metaverse-marketing/634450/.

3 Page, D., 4 Nov. 2017. What happens to your brain when you binge-watch a TV series. *Better*. Retrieved from https://www.nbcnews.com/better/health/what-happens-your-brain-when-you-binge-watch-tv-series-ncna816991.

4 Santiago, E., 21 Jan. 2023. The creator economy market size is grow-ing: How brands can leverage it [blog]. HubSpot. Retrieved from https://blog.hubspot.com/marketing/creator-economy-market-size.

CHAPTER 7: WORK ON YOUR COMMUNITY JOURNEY

1 Rossi, C., 15 Feb. 2020. Why an emotional connection matters in customer loyalty and how to achieve it [blog]. Oracle. Retrieved from https://blogs.oracle.com/marketingcloud/post/why-an-emotional-connection-matters-in-loyalty-and-how-to-achieve-it.

2 Sprout Social, n.d. #BrandsGetReal: What consumers want from brands in a divided society. Retrieved from https://sproutsocial.com/insights/data/social-media-connection/.

CHAPTER 8: DON'T HATE, COLLABORATE

1 TurnTo Networks, 19 Jun. 2017. New study shows user-generated content tops marketing tactics by influencing 90 percent of shop-pers' purchasing decisions. *PR Newswire*. Retrieved from https://www.prnewswire.com/news-releases/new-study-shows-user-generated-content-tops-marketing-tactics-by-influencing-90-percent-of-shoppers-purchasing-decisions-300475348.html.

2 Chitrakorn, K., 9 Aug. 2021. Meet the 'genuinfluencers' who don't want to sell you anything. *Vogue Business*. Retrieved from https://www.voguebusiness.com/companies/meet-the-genuinfluencers-who-dont-want-to-sell-you-anything.

CHAPTER 9: COMMUNITY MANAGEMENT

1 Fazio, L. K., Pillai, R. M. and Patel, D., 2022. The effects of repetition on belief in naturalistic settings. *Journal of Experimental Psychology: General*, *151*(10), pp. 2604–13.

2 Matthew, 2 Nov. 2016. The value of a resend campaign, by the numbers. Mailchimp. Retrieved from https://mailchimp.com/en-gb/resources/the-value-of-a-resend-campaign-by-the-numbers/.

3 Butler, S., 1 Feb. 2022. Marks & Spencer and Aldi call truce in Colin the Caterpillar cake war. *Guardian*. Retrieved from https://www.theguardian.com/business/2022/feb/01/marks-spencer-and-aldi-call-truce-in-colin-the-caterpillar-cake-war.

4 @AldiUK, 17 Oct. 2022. Us next . . . Twitter. Retrieved from https://twitter.com/AldiUK/status/1581963274459176961?lang=en-GB.

5 NWO, 27 May 2009. Half of your friends lost in seven years, social network study finds. ScienceDaily. Retrieved from https://www.sciencedaily.com/releases/2009/05/090527111907.htm.

6 CBC News, 2 Aug. 2006. Novelty 'its own reward' for brain. Retrieved from https://www.cbc.ca/news/science/novelty-its-own-reward-for-brain-1.582020.

7 American Psychological Association, 29 Oct. 2015. Frequently monitoring progress toward goals increases chance of success. ScienceDaily. Retrieved from https://www.sciencedaily.com/releases/2015/10/151029101349.htm#:~:text=Your%20chances%20of%20success%20are,publicly%20or%20physically%20record%20it.&text=FULL%20STORY-,If%20you%20are%20trying%20to%20achieve%20a%20goal%2C%20the%20more,by%20the%20American%20Psychological%20Association.

8 CBC News, 2 Aug. 2006. Novelty 'its own reward' for brain. Retrieved from https://www.cbc.ca/news/science/novelty-its-own-reward-for-brain-1.582020.

9 Actionable Insights, 29 Jan. 2021. Why brand transparency is essential to driving customer loyalty in 2021. Emarsys. Retrieved from https://emarsys.com/learn/blog/why-brand-transparency-is-essential-to-driving-customer-loyalty-in-2021/.

CHAPTER 10: KEEP YOUR CREATIVE JUICES FLOWING

1 Wong, M., 24 Apr. 2014. Stanford study finds walking improves creativity. Stanford News. Retrieved from https://news.stanford.edu/2014/04/24/walking-vs-sitting-042414/.

2 Tabaka, M., 17 Sep. 2015. A surprising way to increase your productivity. *Inc*. Retrieved from https://www.inc.com/marla-tabaka/a-surprising-way-to-increase-your-productivity.html.

3 Iny, D., 1 Aug. 2017. Woody Allen said show up to succeed. Is this what he meant? *Inc*. Retrieved from https://www.inc.com/danny-iny/woody-allen-said-show-up-to-succeed-is-this-what-h.html.

FINAL NOTE

1 Zhou, M., 10 Nov. 2022. How to nurse a vulnerability hangover, according to Brené Brown. Refinery29. Retrieved from https://www.refinery29.com/en-gb/vulnerability-hangover.

INDEX

ABOUT THE AUTHOR

Image Credit: MXH.PHOTOS

Daisy Morris is a social media strategist and Founder of social media consultancy and online community, The Selfhood. She is also a TEDx speaker, workshop host and presenter. Clients and collaborators of Daisy range from tech companies such as Meta, Microsoft and Adobe, to mental health organisations such as Mind and The Self Space. Daisy is also a guest lecturer at universities such as London College of Fashion and The Fashion Retail Academy.

books to help you live a good life

Join the conversation and tell
us how you live a #goodlife

🐦 @yellowkitebooks
📘 YellowKiteBooks
📌 Yellow Kite Books
📷 YellowKiteBooks